A Beginner's Guide to Celtic Spirituality

An Introduction to Celtic Mysteries, Myths, and Rituals

Neve Sullivan

Intrepidas Publishing

CONTENTS

Introduction

Celtic spirituality is the spirituality of the edge of the world. It's the spirituality that stands on windswept rocky shores, gazing westward to the open, stormy sea. It acknowledges that "edge" place in our hearts where time meets eternity, where words fade off into silence, and where heaven silently gazes into the turmoil of earthly life.

–Carl McColman

THIS IS THE FIRST in a series of books on Celtic wisdom for modern life. The goal of the collection is to foster a sense of continuity with the past, to develop an appreciation for ancient wisdom to help us in our lives today, and to emphasize the importance of community. It aims to establish a link with the therapeutic aspects of Celtic wisdom, including new respect for and connection with the natural world.

In the last 300 years, an enormous Scottish, Irish, and Welsh diaspora emigrated to the New World to escape famine and poverty. Now, their descendants seek to understand their Celtic roots and deepen their connection to their ancestral past. Regardless of whether or not we personally claim Celtic ancestry, many of us are drawn to the elements and symbols inherent in Celtic spirituality and seek to understand it. We may, like so many in the modern world, feel a sense of exile from an actual or metaphorical homeland, where the dense forests whisper sacred secrets of wisdom and wonder. Living in modern, urban settings, our very bones eventually begin to dry out if we our surrounded only by a parched desert of concrete, man-made structures, with no iota of green, and when we engage only in humdrum, mundane activities that do not slake our deep thirst for meaning. We are not meant to simply plod along in a world devoid of artistic inspiration, disconnected from our own creative depths and from the natural world. We are meant to mine the deep seams of connection with our roots, to hold our heads up with an alert presence and sniff at the air to catch a whiff of magic.

These books intend to turn to this ancient past to help and inform people who are looking for a deeper meaning in life. By understanding the roots of Celtic culture, it is possible to apply that knowledge to modern life.

The demands of the everyday can be so overwhelming that we lose touch with our instinctual natures and our ancient origins. How do we get back to a relationship with nature and wisdom? Below, we consider how we might do just that.

Our Connection to Nature

If we live in exile from from the natural world, and any sense of the sacred, or deeper meaning in life, then vital parts of our deepest selves begin to wither. What may start as irritability, or a vague discontent and ennui, can lead into a more serious depression if we do nothing to staunch this loss of life essence. When this is the case, we have forgotten where we came from, and the only remedy is to dig the moist, loamy soil, with our bare hands if need be, to get back to our roots – our connection with the wild, sleeping out under the stars until we have reacquainted ourselves with both the light and the shadow side of our lives. The ancient Celts understood this, and it formed an intrinsic part of their spirituality.

As humans, we generally believe that we are the most important beings on Earth. This is damaging and harmful, as our belief in our importance has disconnected us from our natural environment. Because of our exceptionalist mindset, biologist Edward O. Wilson suggests that we are, as a species, "contemptuous towards lower forms of life" (Wilson, 2017: 1). Such attitudes are dangerous, and they threaten our very survival.

In recent times, due to colonial redistribution of people, habitat loss, climate change, and pollution, we have left no ecosystem free from our damaging influence. All of this has been caused by humanity's disregard for its environment (Lynch, 2023).

Daily, most of us do not intentionally harm the natural surroundings in which we live. However, we often fail to appreciate the beauty and importance of the world.

Have you ever walked through a forest, engrossed in your phone, failing to take notice of the earthly beauty that surrounds you? Maybe you have been on a walk along a beautiful beach and were more concerned about taking pictures to show to all your friends on Instagram. Instead, you could have been appreciating the wonder of your surroundings in the here and now.

By contrast, the ancient Celts, who lived in Iron Age Europe between 700 B.C.E. and 400 A.D., lived harmoniously within their environment and considered it to be sacred. They believed that the land possessed powerful spiritual energy. In their religion, they regarded certain natural parts of the landscape, such as river sources, springs, and groves, to be sacred (Cartwright, 2021a). They also believed in animism, the concept that all things in the natural world possess a spirit or a soul. This includes humans and animals, as well as plants, rivers, and rocks (Hugh, 2023).

In the Celtic religion, sacred places were often adorned with purpose-built temples, shrines, and sanctuaries. Here, Druids performed rituals and prayers. Offerings of precious goods alongside animal and human sacrifices as gifts to the Celtic gods were made to gain their favor and secure the continued success of the community (Cartwright, 2021a).

Animal and human sacrifice is a step too far in the modern world, but these examples are clear evidence that the Celts did not take nature for granted.

They revered every tree that they passed rather than accepting each one as a taken-for-granted part of the landscape. Although today we may have lost the belief that trees are sacred, we can still appreciate them and pay them more attention than we do now.

Understanding Celtic Spirituality

Before we explore how Celtic spirituality is relevant to our lives today, we must understand what it is, its origins, and what historical sources concerning it survive.

Historical Roots of Celtic Spirituality

The Celts, or Keltoi, as they were known in Greek, were first defined as such by the ancient Greeks before 500 B.C.E. (Green, 2011). It was around this time that the Greek geographer Hecataeus of Miletus first mentioned them. By that point, the Celts were a common cultural grouping that existed throughout Europe, united by a similar language and common customs.

It's likely the tribes that the Greeks encountered in the early sixth century B.C.E. had been in their territories and speaking Celtic languages since as early as the late Bronze Age (1300–800 B.C.E.) or even earlier (Waldman & Mason, 2006). For the most part, the Celts are considered to have existed during the Iron Age period, which spanned from 1100 B.C.E.–300 A.D. This was the last prehistoric period before Classical writers recorded history.

Before the expansion of ancient Rome and the Germanic and Slavic-speaking tribes, a significant part of Europe was dominated by Celtic cultures, including those in southern Germany, the Czech Republic, and parts of Spain and Portugal (Alberro, 2005). All these countries were designated such as they shared a Celtic language and common cultural and religious traditions.

Today, only six nations or regions in Northwestern Europe are commonly cited as Celtic countries. This is due to the survival of the culture, traditions, and languages in these areas, which had declined in most areas of Europe in the Early Middle Ages. These present regions are Brittany in northwestern France, Cornwall in southwest England, Ireland, Isle of Man, Scotland, and Wales. Parts of the northern Iberian Peninsula, such as modern Galicia, Asturias, Cantabria, and northern Portugal also claim a Celtic heritage, as supported by ancient texts, folklore, and music of the region.

Celtic paganism is derived from its practice in the Proto-Indo-European region, as evidenced by the fact that many deities found in Celtic myth correspond with those that exist in other Indo-European mythologies. For example, the Celtic goddess Brigantia corresponds with the Roman Aurora while Irish Danu is the same deity as the Hindu Danu, and the Welsh Arianrhod serves the same role as the Greek goddess Selene (Mallory & Adams, 2006).

Figures who held exceptional importance were Druids, who played an important role in the religious practices of the Celts. They are often considered to be the priests of the religion but, in reality, they were involved in politics, prophecy, ritual sacrifice, and the control of the supernatural world. They preserved the oral religious tradition, acted as teachers, and served as royal advisors. In some instances, they were rulers themselves. Their followers often venerated and feared them, as they believed the priests could communicate with the divine world.

In Book VI of his *Commentaries: On the Gallic War*, Julius Caesar describes their role as follows (Green, 1997: 10):

> Throughout Gaul, there are two classes of men of some dignity and importance ... One of the two classes is that of the Druids, the other that of the knights. The Druids are concerned with the worship of the gods, look after public and private sacrifice, and expound religious matters. A large number of young men flock to them for training and hold them in high honor. For they have the right to decide nearly all public and private disputes and they also pass judgment and decide rewards and penalties in criminal and murder cases and disputes concerning legacies and boundaries.

Caesar's observations suggest that the Druids' function was both as religious and secular authority figures. This implies that boundaries between the two were far more fluid than they are in the modern world.

After the Roman Empire conquered Gaul (58–51 B.C.E.) and South Britain (48 B.C.E.), the Celtic religion underwent some Romanization, leading to the emergence of a syncretic Gallo-Roman religion with deities such as Mars Lenus, Apollo Grannus, and Telesphorus, which were combinations of Celtic and Roman gods and goddesses (Green, 1997). By the first century A.D., Celtic culture had adopted Roman forms of expression, but its societies retained their names for deities and traditional worship still took place occasionally. Archaeological evidence for this includes the bronze cross-legged statuette from Bouray-sur-Juine and the wooden sculptures from the Sources de la Seine (King, 1990).

It was not until the second century A.D. that the Roman names for gods became more commonplace. This shift was likely related to a decline in the Celtic side of the Romano-Celtic religion. In turn, this may be linked to a lessening of the use of the Celtic language, particularly among those rich enough to have an inscription carved. It is impossible to be certain about the general extent of the language change. Notably though, by the fourth century A.D., most references to deities in Gaul were by their Roman names. From this evidence, it seems that the Romano-Celtic religion had become a regional variant of the Empire-wide classical cults.

Toward the end of the Roman period, the Celtic religion declined as Europe slowly converted to Christianity between the third and fifth centuries A.D. It's possible that the reduced influence of the Celtic or Romano-Celtic religion cleared the path for the advance of Christianity across Europe from the fourth century onward. By the fifth century A.D., only the most remote shrines to the ancient religion survived, signaling its end (King, 1990).

Death and the Afterlife in Celtic Spirituality

The Celts believed in life after death, so they buried food, weapons, and ornaments with the deceased. Tombs contained an entire range of objects, from tools to jewelry, indicating that the departed person was expected to go on a journey and that they would need the items buried with them when they reached their ultimate destination (Niemchick & Rogers, 2023; Cartwright, 2021b).

The Irish Celts believed in an Otherworld, which was sometimes envisioned as being underground or an island in the sea. This place was known as the "Land of the Living," the "Delightful Plain," the "Land of the Young," and *Tír na nÓg* in Irish (Niemchick & Rogers, 2023). Many stories and legends grew around the analogy of transitioning from one place to another.

In essence, the Otherworld was a series of different lands, meaning that there was no one word used to describe where individuals would go after death. Believers thought that this was a place where there was no sickness, old age, or death, where happiness lasted forever, and where a day lasted for 100 years. It was similar to the Elysium of the Greeks, and the concept may come from a more general Indo-European tradition.

In Christianity, the belief in a state of existence beyond our present one is simplified into the opposing binary ideas of Heaven/Paradise and Hell, with believers expecting to go to one or another of these realms after death. Which one they would go to would depend on whether they behaved well or badly in life. However, the Celtic concept of the next world does not see a person's behavior on Earth as defining where they go after death. Instead, it seems that the individual could end up in various possible lives or could encounter different other worlds by chance and even return to normal life afterward (Heinz, 2010).

One example of this is found in the Irish-Celtic vision or voyage stories. In such tales, a beautiful girl approaches the hero and sings to him of a happy land (the Otherworld). He follows her and, either, they sail away in a boat of glass and are never seen again, or he returns after what he believes to be a short amount of time only to find that, because he has been away for hundreds of years, all his companions are dead (Niemchick & Rogers, 2023).

The above story demonstrates how the Celts believed that people could wander through different worlds. Notably, afterlife locations were not exclusive or restrictive. Humans and the inhabitants of the Otherworld could interact with one another, and they could even travel between their alternate realms and back as they pleased (Heinz, 2010). Such movements were possible due to the existence of what were called "thin places." This is a Celtic term for "those locales where the distance between Heaven and Earth collapses" (Burkeman, 2014). This means that, in this belief system, it is possible to sense or even access alternative realms.

Their belief in the Otherworld meant that the Celts felt that they had little to fear from death—it was simply an extension of life. The lack of division seen between our world and the afterlife also indicates that there was nothing to fear from dying. Rather, it was simply another part of life. In Celtic tradition, after people die, they go on a voyage to the afterlife. This is symbolic of the need to stay open to new experiences. In present times, we can learn from this by striving to stay open to new experiences in the same way that the Celts did.

Other of their traditions around death included saying prayers and blessings for the dead. The Druids also taught the doctrine of the transmigration of souls and that the soul departs from the head (Niemchick & Rogers, 2023; Cartwright, 2021b).

Another significant aspect of Celtic spirituality in life was that it encouraged individuals to forge strong connections with one another. One example of this is the concept of "Anam Cara," which refers to the Celtic spiritual belief of souls bonding and connecting. The popular late Irish poet and philosopher John O'Donohue's bestselling book, titled *Anam Cara* (1996), explores this concept in depth. In this spiritual tradition, your soul radiates all around your physical body like an aura. When you connect with another person and become completely open and trusting with that individual, your two beings begin to flow together. Should such a deep bond be formed, you have found your Anam Cara, or soulmate (Whitaker, 2023). The concept thus encourages us to cherish our relationships as deeply as the Celts did.

Compared to modern times, Celtic beliefs around the afterlife and human bonds are less binary. Today, we are inclined to see life and death as entirely separate from one another. The Celts, on the other hand, saw death as a continuation of life and as a state of living rather than a definitive end. In the West, we often fear and avoid the topic of dying, as if it didn't exist. By way of contrast, the Celts were at peace with the concept, accepting it as an integral part of existence.

Sacred Presences in the Celtic World

The Celts perceived their world as brimming with sacred presence. They saw divinity mirrored not only in heroic men but also in women, animals, trees, and rivers—even rocks held a spark of the divine. Unlike Greek and

Roman society, which was predominately urban, Celtic society revolved around rural life. As such, it enjoyed a close link with the natural world that is demonstrated by the spirits its adherents worshipped, which were those of both the wild and cultivated landscapes and their inhabitants.

The Celtic religion focused on the features of the landscape, waters, forests, and animals. Additionally, because divine power was associated with the fertility of humans, livestock, and crops, these objects were venerated. Tribal territories were held sacred, and the ground that received the bodies of the dead was seen as holy and revered by living relatives. Celts invoked the spirits of water-related places, as these bodies were givers of life and a link between the earthly and other worlds.

Furthermore, celestial powers, especially the sun and thunder, were acknowledged as divine and sought out by those seeking favors from deities. Notably, inscribed dedications and iconography dating from the Roman period show that these spirits were perceived as personifications of natural features (Green, 1997).

Classical writings suggest that, while the Celts worshipped the forms of natural objects, they did not consider their deities in anthropomorphic terms (Wood, 2000). For example, Sequana *was* the spring source of the Seine, not just its human representative, as Sulis *was* the hot spring at bath, and Taranis *was* thunder. Similarly, Celtic spirits were close to the animals they were associated with. The names of Artio, the bear goddess, and Epona, the horse goddess, are based on the Gaulish words for "bear" and "horse," respectively. This shows how the Celts worshipped nature itself, not human versions of natural forces.

Evidence of the Celtic Religion

Before we proceed, a word of caution is needed about the surviving primary-source evidence concerning the Celtic religion. Because most Iron Age Celts were illiterate, we have no surviving information about the religion from those who practiced it. Instead, information about the beliefs and nature of the Celtic belief system comes from ancient literature, such as Roman commentaries on the Celts and the vernacular mythic sources of Ireland and Wales. Facts about the Celtic religion can also be gleaned from archaeological findings, especially from the Roman period, when inscribed dedications and religious images were commonplace and contributed to our knowledge of this subject.

All surviving sources of information on the Celtic religion need to be treated with caution for the following reasons. First, Roman historians were inherently biased, and their works often included distortions, expressed ignorance and misunderstandings of Celtic culture, displayed literary conventions, and stereotyped the Celts as "barbaric" (Green, 1997). These factors mean that the picture Roman sources present is often wildly inaccurate.

Meanwhile, early Welsh and Irish vernacular sources on the Celtic religion were written hundreds of years after the Celtic period, when most of Europe had converted to Christianity. This means that the views on the old pagan religion expressed may be biased. It may be that some specific texts do contain genuine echoes or resonances of the pre-Christian past. However, the earliest mythic stories of Ireland and Wales, such as those contained in the *Mabinogi* (Wales) and "The Táin" (part of the Irish *Ulster Cycle*) were not compiled in written form until the Medieval period (Green, 1997). Opinion is divided as to whether these texts contain material derived from oral tradition or whether they are a creation of their Medieval monastic curators.

While the archaeological evidence does not contain the bias present in literary sources, understanding of these artifacts is informed by a 21st-century mindset (Green, 1997). This means that we may fail to understand and appreciate the true meaning of surviving materials relating to the ancient Celtic religion.

What to Expect From This Book

This book will provide a detailed exploration of Celtic spirituality and how to adapt and apply some of this ancient wisdom to our lives today. Throughout five chapters and a conclusion, it will offer you a broad overview of Celtic culture, its history, its influences, how it relates to the present, and what hope it can offer us for the future.

Following this introductory section, Chapter 1, "Celtic Mythology and Ritual," presents explanations of key aspects of Celtic mythology, exploring the legends behind popular figures in this belief system, such as Cernunnos, the Morrígan, and Brigid, as well as less-well-known Celtic deities.

Chapter 2, titled "Nature and Landscape," elaborates on how the Celts revered nature and saw divinity in all its natural elements, such as trees, rivers, and mountains. Here, we will also look at how Celtic folklore and belief in fairies relate to the natural world and their relationship to trees and forests. This chapter will also present an overview of sites sacred to this ancient society and landscapes and modern pilgrimages to these sites.

We explore the Celts' special relationship with animals in Chapter 3: The Animal Kingdom.

In the fourth chapter, "The Divine Feminine in the Celtic Tradition," we consider the importance and role of women in this spiritual tradition as well as examples of female warriors and leaders who lived during that period.

The Arts as Sacred (Chapter 5) discusses how the arts enjoyed an elevated status in Celtic cultures. Examples include the spoken-word tradition of storytelling and poetry, the visual arts, including cave art and illustrations found in sacred texts, the written word, including ogham, the ancient script used by the Celts, dance, and song.

The concluding chapter then presents key takeaways gleaned from this exploration of this topic. So, if you want to learn more about Celtic spirituality and culture, read on!

Chapter One

Celtic Mythology and Ritual

All the stream that's roaring by
Came out of a needle's eye

–W.B. Yeats, from "A Needle's Eye"

Due to the lack of written sources by the Celts themselves, we cannot know for certain how, when, and why the Celtic religion began. What we do know is that the Celtic peoples of Western Europe had intricate networks of myths, rituals, and gods that were made up of many of the same figures that were worshipped in similar ways in different cultural contexts.

The goal of this chapter is to help you make sense of Celtic mythology, rituals, gods, goddesses, and belief systems. You will be introduced to various myths related to Celtic culture, including those concerning deities, heroes, and mystical creatures. We have also included references to lesser-known Celtic deities to help you develop a comprehensive understanding of this religion.

In addition to the above, in closing the chapter, we will consider the connection between Celtic mythology and spirituality as well as ways to integrate its spiritual rituals and practice into everyday, modern life.

Celtic Mythology

Celtic mythology refers to the tales and legends of the Celtic people. Most surviving Celtic lore belongs to the Insular Celts, comprised of the Gauls of Scotland and Ireland and the Celtic Britons of western Britain and Brittany.

The Celts did have a written language. In his *Commentarii de Bello Gallico*, Julius Caesar confirms this by reporting that the Helvetii had a written census (2022, 1.29). Most Celtic writings, historians assume, were destroyed by the Romans, and Caesar also notes that the Druids were forbidden from using writing to record certain verses of religious significance. These were presumably too sacred to be written down (Chadwick, 1970).

Nevertheless, some Celtic mythology survived the Roman occupation and the Dark Ages through oral lore. Christians in the Middle Ages eventually recorded these legends in writing, albeit without the original religious meanings (Ross, 1972). For example, early Irish and Welsh texts were recorded by Christian scribes who were often hostile to the "pagan" traditions of the past, so they removed material considered to be improper or offensive from the tales (Ellis, 1999).

The Christian scribes reduced the roles of the gods in the myths they recorded to shadowy phantoms, or they transformed the deities into kings, queens, or heroes. Examples include Conchobar mac Nessa or Rhiannon. Similarly, Druids were transformed into wizards or sorcerers.

Notably, Lugh Lamhfada, or Lugh the Long-Handed, the senior of the gods and patron of arts and crafts, was eventually demoted to Lugh-Chromain, "Stooping Lugh," which translates in modern-day English to "leprechaun" (Ellis, 1999). Through such means, the most senior of the gods was reduced to a faintly ridiculous imaginary creature.

The largest surviving written body of myths comes from Ireland, followed by Wales, with some myths from other Celtic cultures also being known to us in the present day. Each is discussed in detail below. However, we should bear in mind that, because the original material and meaning were removed from many Celtic texts, some scholars have argued that our knowledge of Celtic mythology is highly fragmentary (Ellis, 1999).

It is also worth noting that the myths of Ireland and Wales were written in the vernacular (Welsh or Irish), rather than in Latin, indicating that these stories were native to the countries they were recorded in, rather than a facet of the dominant Christian European culture that dominated in the medieval period (Green, 1997).

Irish Mythology

Most Celtic mythology that survives into the present day comes from Irish lore. These stories and legends were originally passed down through word-of-mouth during the prehistoric period. Later on, during the early medieval period, many Celtic myths from Ireland were written down by Christian scribes, who modified and Christianized the stories to varying degrees.

The Irish myths are grouped into four "cycles" as explored below:

The Mythological Cycle

The *Mythological Cycle* also known as *The Cycle of the Gods* was compiled in the 12th century A.D. (Green, 1997). It contains tales and poems about mythological races, including the Tuatha Dé Danann, many of which are thought to represent Irish deities.

When scribes recorded these myths, the gods were recast as kings, queens, Druids, bards, warriors, heroes, healers, and craftsmen with supernatural powers. Based on what survives in *The Mythological Cycle*, it is apparent that the chief god was the Dagda ("the great god") while the Morrígan ("the great queen" or "phantom queen") was a triple goddess associated with sovereignty, war, and fate. Other gods featured in this cycle include Lugh, Nuada, Aengus, Brigid, Manannán, Dian Cécht, the healer, and Goibniu, the smith, one of the Tri Dé Dana ("three gods of craft").

In this cycle, the traditional rivals to the gods are the Fomorians, or Fomoire, a monstrous people whom the Tuatha Dé Danann defeat in the Cath Maige Tuired ("Battle of Moytura"). *The Mythological Cycle* also contains other important works of Celtic mythology of Irish origin, such as the "Aided Chlainne Lir" ("Children of Lir") and the "Lebor Gabála Érenn" ("Book of Invasions"), a legendary history of Ireland.

The Ulster Cycle

The *Ulster Cycle* of prose tales was recorded in writing sometime between the 7th and 12th centuries, although it probably came from a much earlier oral tradition that contains what are arguably the earliest vernacular mythic texts (Green, 1997). This cycle includes the heroic legends about the Ulaid, focusing on the mythological Ulster king, Conchobar Mac Nessa, and his court located at Emain Macha, the hero Cú Chulainn, and their war with the Connachta and Queen Medb. The longest and most significant tale included in *The Ulster Cycle* is the epic "Táin Bó Cúailnge" ("Cattle Raid of Cooley").

The Fianna Cycle

The *Fianna Cycle* or *Fenian Cycle* was compiled in the 12th century and revolves around the exploits of Finn, a mythical hero, and his group of warriors, the Fianna. This cycle includes the long epic "Acallam na Senórach" ("Tales of the Elders").

The Kings' Cycle

The Kings' Cycle is made up of legends about historical and semi-mythological kings of Ireland as well as stories about the origins of the people and dynasties of the land. One example is the "Buile Shuibhne" ("The Madness of King Sweeny").

Irish mythology also includes Celtic mythical texts that do not fit into any of the four cycles. Examples include the "Dindsenchas" ("Lore of Places") and the tales of journeys to the Otherworld (such as "The Voyage of Brân"). As a lot of written material has not survived into the present day, many more Irish myths once existed but are lost to us now.

Welsh Mythology

What is known to us about Welsh mythology comes from three key manuscripts that were created in the medieval period. These are *Llyfr du Caefyrddin* or *The Black Book of Carmarthen* (ca. 1250), *Llyfr Gwyn Rhydderch* or *The White Book of Rhydderch* (ca. 1325), and *Llyfr Coch Hergest* or *The Red Book of Hergest* (ca. 1382–1410). Dispersed through these books are manuscript copies of the four branches of the "Mabinogi," the most highly regarded cycle of British prose literature and the main source of information about Welsh-origin Celtic mythology.

These manuscripts and the mythology contained within survive today thanks to the efforts of Lady Charlotte Guest (1812–1895), a wealthy aristocrat with an interest in early Welsh literature, who collected and translated the "Mabinogi" along with several unrelated medieval tales and romances from the same sources in her *Mabinogion* (1838–1849; MacKillop, 2004).

The Mabinogion is a collection of early-medieval Welsh vernacular tales, which were compiled in written form in the 10th century and survived in 14th-century manuscripts. These stories are essentially pagan, indicating that they contain references to pre-Christian myths and beliefs (Green, 1997).

The *Pedeir Keinc y Mabinogi* ("Four Branches of the Mabinogi") comprise four stories that are separate but related and are the primary source of several significant characters that feature heavily in Celtic mythology, including Rhiannon, Teyrnon, and Brân the Blessed (Bendigeidfran "Brân [Crow] the Blessed").

The most important aspect of the Brân myth involves his wonderous severed head. The tale states that the giant was mortally wounded and requested that his companions cut off his head and take it with them on their travels. In asking this of them, he hoped that they would be provided with entertainment and companionship.

Along their journey, Brân's companions would remain uncorrupted as long as they avoided opening a certain forbidden door. If they failed to do this, they would return to the real world and be reminded of their sorrows. All this happened as Brân said it would, and those mentioned in the story passed 80 joyful years. The head was later buried in London, where it kept away all invaders from Britain until it was finally dug up (The Editors of Encyclopaedia Britannica, 2024b).

Other characters that feature in *The Mabinogion* have their origins in Proto-Indo-European mythology. Examples include Lleu Llaw Gyffes, the hero who cannot be killed except in seemingly contradictory circumstances, and Arawn, a king of the Otherworld who seeks the aid of a mortal in his feuds (Miller, 1998).

Surviving Welsh myths do help explain the significance of Celtic religious symbols such as cauldrons. For example, in "The Second Branch," there is a description of a magical cauldron that comes from an Irish lake that illustrates the role of cauldrons in Celtic spirituality. In this instance, the object has the power to bring dead warriors to life, although their continued inability to speak indicates that they are still, in a sense, dead and that they belong to the Otherworld (Green, 1997).

Although there are many similarities between Welsh and Irish mythology, it is unlikely that there was any unified British mythological tradition.

Other Celtic Mythologies

There were numerous Celtic gods, so in some cases, it is inevitable that only their names would have survived. In addition to them, Classical writers have also preserved some fragments of myths or legends that may be Celtic in origin. For example, the Syrian rhetorician, Lucian, claimed that Ogmios was the leader of a band of men chained by their ears to his tongue. This was meant to symbolize the strength of his eloquence (Oxford Reference, 2024).

Meanwhile, the first-century Roman poet, Lucan, mentions the gods Taranis ("Thunderer"), Teutates ("God of the People"), and Esus ("Lord" or "Master"). Later commentators have claimed that Esus's victims were sacrificed by being ritually stabbed and hung from trees and that all three gods required appeasement through human sacrifice (Green, 1997). To this end, a relief from the Cathedral of Notre Dame in Paris portrays Esus as a bent woodman cutting a branch from a willow tree (The Editors of Encyclopaedia Britannica, 2024a). However, there is no evidence that Taranis, Teutates, and Esus were important Celtic deities.

Other fragments from Celtic myth may be found in surviving objets d'art, coins, and altars. Historians have suggested that these artifacts depict scenes from lost myths. Examples include representations of Tarvos Trigaranus, or of an equestrian believed to be Jupiter, climbing on top of the anguiped (a snake-legged, human-like figure). The Gundestrup cauldron may also refer to lost myths (Olmsted, 1976).

Some names of Celtic gods have survived in the form of dedications. For example, a stone altar found in Böckingen, Germany included an inscribed dedication to Taranucnus, a derivative of Taranis, the Celtic god of thunder, one of the three gods mentioned by Lucan as requiring appeasement through human sacrifice (Green, 1997).

Some deity representations come with no name. For example, a bronze statue of a figure wearing armor was found in Saint-Maur-en-Chaussée, France. This figure is assumed to be a Celtic warrior god, but the absence of a dedication or a sacred context may suggest that he instead represents a local chieftain rather than a deity (Green, 1997). This example shows how difficult it is to work out the purpose of some surviving Celtic artifacts.

There are deity representations with no name that have been discovered in modern times that are likely to be depictions of gods. Examples include images of a three-headed or three-faced god, one that is squatting, one with a snake, another with a wheel, and a horseman placed next to a kneeling giant (Powell, 1958). Some of these images have been discovered preserved in Late Bronze Age peat bogs in Britain, suggesting that the symbols pre-date Roman times and that they were commonplace across Celtic culture (Chadwick, 1970).

Beyond this, the distribution of these images indicates that they were most likely attached to certain tribes and were distributed from some central point of communal settlement outward along trade routes. For example, the image of the three-headed god emerges from among the Belgae, an ancient Celtic people that lived in northern Gaul between the Oise, Marne, and Moselle rivers. Meanwhile, the horseman with the kneeling giant originates from either side of the Rhine. These instances demonstrate that certain images depict locally worshipped gods with mythologies that have since been lost.

Gods and Goddesses

Evidence of Celtic deities and how they were worshipped survives from the Roman period. Some information about the Celtic gods and goddesses of Gaul comes from Caesar's history of the Gallic War, titled *Commentarii de Bello Gallico* (2022). In this text, Caesar names the five principal gods worshipped in Gaul, giving them the names of the closest equivalent Roman gods, and describing their roles in Celtic myth and culture. Other evidence survives in the form of images that represent the deities and inscribed dedications that have been found across the Celtic world (Green, 1997).

According to Caesar, Mercury was the most venerated of all the Celtic deities, something that is proven by the fact that numerous representations of him have been discovered. This god was seen as the originator of the arts, the supporter of trade and adventurers, and the primary decider of profit. Next, the Gauls revered Apollo, Mars, Jupiter, and Minerva, with these deities seen as being of equal importance across the Celtic world. Apollo cured sickness, Minerva encouraged the development of skills, Jupiter governed the skies, and Mars influenced warfare.

Caesar also mentions that the Gauls traced their ancestry back to Dis Pater, also known as Rex Infernus or Pluto, the god of the underworld (Ross, 1972). According to Caesar, "The Gauls claim that they are all descended from Dis Pater: they say that this is the tradition handed down to them from the Druids" (Cunliffe, 1997: 277). As Dis Pater was the god of the dead, he was the first man alive and the first to die. Thus, he acquired control of the underworld.

In Irish mythology, the five main gods are believed to be equivalent to:

- Manannán mac Lir (Mercury)

- Lugh (Apollo; however, most sources believe Lugh to be equivalent to Mercury)

- The Dagda (Jupiter)

- Neit (Mars)

- Brigid (Minerva)

Certain deities were widely venerated across the Celtic world; meanwhile, others were limited to a single region or even a specific locality. Several supra-regional cults flourished across Celtic tribal boundaries, albeit with regional variations. Examples include the Matres (mother goddesses), Cernunnos (the "horned one" and the "lord of wild things"), the god of thunder, Taranis, and Epona, the goddess of horses (Green, 1997; Editors of Encyclopaedia Britannica, 2023b).

However, most Celtic deities were extremely localized, sometimes occurring at just one shrine. In some cases, this is because the spirit was a genius loci, the governing spirit of a particular place. In Gaul alone, over 400 different Celtic deity names are recorded, at least 300 of which occur just once. For example, Sulis belonged to Bath, Sequana was confined to the spring shrine near Dijon, and the war deities Cocidius and Belatucadros were each worshipped in clearly defined territories in the area of Hadrian's Wall (Green, 1997).

Notably, certain local or regional deities were often more popular in their area than the supra-regional deities were. For example, in east-central Gaul, the local healing goddess, Sequana, who was located at a spring near Dijon in modern-day Burgundy, was probably more influential in the minds of local devotees than the Matres, who were worshipped all over Britain, Gaul, and the Rhineland (Green, 1997).

Several separate deity types occur in Celtic mythology. Some examples are:

- **Antlered deities**: Such as Cerannos and others. This is a recurrent figure in Gaulish iconology. Antlered deities are frequently depicted as cross-legged and with antlers. They are sometimes surrounded by animals and often hold a torc.

- **Healing deities**: These are found across the Celtic world and are frequently associated with thermal springs, healing wells, herbalism, and light. The most well-known is Brigid, goddess of healing, poetry, and smithcraft. These deities are associated with hot springs, which the Celts believed to be therapeutic (Green, 2011).

- **Sacred-water deities:** These figures are similar to the healing deities. Examples include Sulis, Sequana, and Brigid.

- **Solar deities**: In ancient Celtic culture, the sun was a feminine force, and several goddesses were possibly solar (Koch, 2006). For example, in Irish mythology, Grian is the winter sun while she is alternatively known as Áine (who is sometimes depicted as her sister), the summer sun (MacKillop, 1998).

- **Horse deities:** As an instrument of Indo-European expansion, the horse was a significant part of the mythologies of all Celtic cultures. The most notable example is the cult of Epona. She was the embodiment of "horsepower" or horsemanship. Because it was vital to the success and survival of the tribe, such power was important.

- **Mother goddesses**: The three Matres were worshipped across the Celtic world as symbols of sovereignty, creativity, birth, fertility, sexual union, and nurturing.

- **Divine couples**: Male and female deities frequently appeared in pairs across the Celtic world and were often worshipped together in this way. Examples include Rosmerta and Mercury, Mars Loucetius and Nemetona, and Sirona and Apollo Grannus (Jufer & Luginbuhl, 2001).

Celtic Spiritual Rituals

Greek and Roman accounts of the Celts make numerous references to assemblies and ceremonies associated with religion or quasi-religious activities. Some of these festivals were annual rituals, such as those associated with the passing of the seasons, while others were more spontaneous and localized in nature.

Drawing on the work of Posidonius, who lived in the first century B.C.E., in *Deipnosophists IV,* Athenaeus tells of a central Gaulish chieftain called Luernius, ruler of the Arverni, who held a festival where "in an attempt to win popular favor, [he] rode in a chariot over the plains, distributing gold and silver to the tens of thousands of Celts who followed him" (Green, 1997: 34). To cap off the festivities, Luernius hosted a large feast that went on for several days. This festival seems more like a celebration or a popularity contest than a religious ritual. However, for the Celts, religious and spiritual concerns were intimately related to the practicalities of daily life.

Another example from Irish vernacular mythic texts refers to politico-religious assemblies and festivals, notably the Great Assembly of Tara (the sacred place of royal investiture) where fairs, markets, horse races, and other social events took place (Green, 1997). This example also emphasizes the ingrained place of spiritual concerns in the daily lives of the Celts.

Early Irish texts also name the four great seasonal festivals, Imbolc, Beltane, Lughnasadh, and Samhain, some of which were strongly associated with the Druids. These festivals marked important points in the farming calendar, and their functions were to appropriate the divine powers for healthy crops and livestock, to mark the passage of the seasons, and to allow the local people to relax after a long, intense period of agricultural labor (Green, 1997). Each of these festivals and their purpose is discussed in detail below:

The Four Main Seasonal Festivals

Imbolc (Spring)

The word *imbolc* means "purification." The festival took place on February 1 and celebrated the lambing season and the lactation of ewes. Its name perhaps came from its association with the pure white of milk. Notably, the alternative name for Imbolc, o*imelc* denotes the time ewes come into milk, which also signifies spring (MacKillop, 2004).

Imbolc was primarily a purification festival, and its purpose may have been to prevent pregnant ewes, their lambs, and their milk from being harmed. The celebration may have its origins in other natural phenomena, such as the obvious lengthening of daylight, an event that anticipates the beginning of spring. The festival was also associated with the pagan Irish fire goddess, Brigid (Green, 1997).

Beltane (Summer)

Beltane (or *Beltain*) derives either from the word *bil* (luck) or *bel* (light). It is the great Celtic May festival, which is still celebrated under this name in Scotland and Ireland. It is known as "Calan Mai" in Wales, "Cetshamain" in Ireland, "Cala'Me" in Cornwall, and "Kala-Hanv" in Brittany (MacKillop, 2004). The festival is celebrated on May 1 (or May 15 in Scotland), and it is the official beginning of summer in the Celtic calendar. In ancient times, this was when livestock was moved onto high pastureland (Green, 1997). The celebration may also derive from the veneration of Belenus (with the Celtic root "bel" meaning "bright"), a god whose cult was associated with health-giving waters.

Beltane, still celebrated in present times, has traditionally been a fire festival. In his *Glossary*, the ninth-century Irish writer Cormac formed a strong link between Beltane and the Druids. He spoke of two great fires being made, between which cattle were driven. This was a symbolic protection against disease (Green, 1997).

It was also a time for ritual eating or for having certain kinds of food. Beltane cake or bannock, still made and eaten today, is large, round, and flat and made from oats and barley. Traditionally, these were large enough to be broken up into several portions, one of which contained a black spot made with charcoal. The person who drew this piece by lot was the Beltane carline or old hag. He or she might be subject to a mock execution involving being thrown into the fire or being drawn and quartered (MacKillop, 2004).

A ritual associated with Beltane and that has continued in Scotland and Ireland into the modern era is May Dew. This involves young ladies going out "a-maying" on May 1 and washing their faces in the first dew of the month. The Celts believed that participating in this tradition guaranteed health and beauty in the forthcoming year (McQuillan, 2024). It was commonly practiced up until the 1970s.

In addition, Beltane was considered to be a good day to start a project. Notably, the Partholónians and the Milesians invaded Ireland on Beltane, according to *Lebor Gabála Érenn*, known in English as *The Book of Invasions* (MacKillop, 2004).

Lughnasadh (Fall)

This was the Celtic harvest festival celebrated on August 1. The festivities from the fortnight before and extended to the fortnight after this date. It was named in honor of the great Irish divinity, Lugh, the god of light, war, and craftsmanship. He was said to have founded the festival in honor of his foster mother, Tailtiu. The gathering also celebrated the ripening of grain (MacKillop, 2004). Lughnasadh was celebrated at various great Irish centers, these being Emain Macha in Ulster, Carman in Leinster, and Tara for the whole of Ireland (Green, 1997).

The *Dindscenchas* describes Lughnasadh as a festival that included an assembly or gathering where political and legal matters were settled. It was also a forum for intertribal games, such as horse racing and martial arts displays as well as feasting. Ritual events to promote a successful harvest would have also taken place here and were likely presided over by Druids and other religious officials (Green, 1997).

Samhain (Winter)

This festival was celebrated on October 31/November 1. The word *samhain* may derive from the Irish word *samrad* or the Gaulish *samon*, terms that refer to the warm season in the Celtic year. Thus, Samhain may have signified the end of the warm weather and the beginning of winter. A great assembly was held at Tara at the time, so the origin of the festival may have been linked to the rounding up and selection of domestic animals for winter culling, food provision, or breeding. Ceremonies associated with sacred kingship were also linked to the winter festival (Green, 1997).

In ancient times, Samhain was also a dangerous time, as is its modern successor, Halloween. It was a period during which the conventional boundaries between space and time were suspended and the spirits of the Otherworld temporarily mingled freely with the living. Consequently, Samhain was a time of great spiritual energy. For this reason, Druids were associated with the festivities as their mediatory powers were required to control the supernatural energy flowing from the open Otherworld (Green, 1997).

The lack of boundaries between the two worlds also meant that the Celts believed significant events to be likely to take place at Samhain. Both the Ulster hero Cú Chulainn and the superhuman war leader Finn of *The Fenian Cycle* had Otherworld encounters at this time. Also, at the festival, the tribal god, the Dagda, mated with the raven war goddess, the Morrígan (Green, 1997).

These examples illustrate how all the great religious festivals were linked to events in the farming calendar and related to agricultural and pastoral activities. This was done in a similar way to the Roman calendar of festivals, which combined ritual observances with celebrations of the different phases of the year (Green, 1997).

Ritual Activity

Some rituals the Celts participated in sound barbaric to us in the present day, but back then, they were seen as necessary to guarantee the fertility of livestock and the prosperity of the community.

One such brutal ritual is recorded by Pliny the Elder in his *Natural History*, written in the first century A.D. During this religious ceremony held in Gaul, the Druids cut down mistletoe that grew upon a sacred oak and then sacrificed two white bulls. They used the shrub cuttings as a cure for infertility (Pliny, *Natural History* XVI, 95 cited in Green, 1997: 18):

> The Druids—that is what they call their magicians—hold nothing more sacred than the mistletoe and a tree on which it is growing, provided it is Valonia Oak ... Mistletoe is rare and when found, it is gathered with great ceremony, particularly on the sixth day of the moon ... Hailing the moon in a native word that means "healing all things," they prepare a ritual sacrifice and banquet beneath a tree and bring up two white bulls, whose horns are bound for the first time on this occasion. A priest arrayed in white vestments climbs the tree and with a golden sickle cuts down the mistletoe, which is caught in a white cloak. Then, finally, they kill the victims, praying to God to render his gift propitious to those on whom he has bestowed it. They believe that mistletoe given in drink will impart fertility to any barren animal and that it is an antidote to all poisons.

This passage shows how the Celtic religion was concerned with healing and fertility. According to Pliny, the Celts used mistletoe as both a healing agent and a fertility aid. The plant can be seen to have had religious or spiritual significance to the Celts, given that it was often used as a motif in early Celtic art. Human heads bearing curious leaf-shaped crowns were a common decoration that was used on jewelry and stone monuments (Green, 1997). The shape of the leaves found on these objects resembles European mistletoe.

Fecundity also played an important part in Celtic religious concerns due to its significance for human and animal life. The ground's ability to provide abundant crops on which communities thrived was also a prominent theme. Divine powers associated with the fertility of humans, livestock, and crops were therefore objects of veneration.

Celtic spirits, such as the Matres, were associated with the fruitfulness of the land. These mothers were responsible for the earth's bounty. They are depicted on altars with baskets of fruit on their laps and accompanied by acolytes bearing garlands of flowers (Green, 1997).

Cauldrons were another symbol of fertility for the Celts, which they associated with inexhaustibility, inspiration, and regeneration, all properties relating to the capacity for bearing new life. Cauldrons were associated with the Dagda, the fertility god, and Ceridwen and Branwen, the goddesses of fertility and love, respectively (MacCulloch et al., 2023).

Some Celtic festivals focused on the fertility of the land. The May festival of Beltane, as mentioned above, included the Druidic fire ritual celebrating the beginning of summer. During the ceremony, cattle were driven between two bonfires as a fertility and purification custom (Green, 1997).

As Pliny's observations suggest, the moon was another important aspect of the Celtic religion and was firmly connected with healing. Other evidence confirms this, such as how Celtic goddesses associated with health and regeneration are sometimes depicted wearing luna amulets. In addition, the great temple to the healer-goddess Sulis Minerva at Bath was adorned with a carving of the Roman moon goddess, Luna (Green, 1997). These examples indicate that the Celts believed that the celestial body played some role in the healing process.

Everyday activity also held ritual significance for the Celts. For example, hunting hares was considered to be sacred. This was perhaps due to the creature's March antics and because they forage at night. In Celtic culture, they were associated with power and military success. Notably, the warrior-queen Boudica is recorded as sacrificing a hare to her goddess of victory, Andraste, in the mid-first century (Green, 1997).

Including Celtic Rituals in Everyday Life

In the Western world, from the 19th century onward, there has been a renewed interest in Celtic culture. This revival originally occurred in the arts and literature, but from the late 20th century onward, it has included the revival of the ancient Celtic religion. As of 2016, Celtic reconstructionism is the third most common form of pagan revivalism in the United States after Asatru (Germanic reconstructionism) and Kemetic reconstructionism (Harris et al., 2016). Although it is popular in America, forms of Celtic revivalism are mostly practiced across Britain and Western Europe (Bonewits, 2006).

As there are no sacred texts associated with the Celtic religion, most modern pagans base their ritual activity on their research, using archaeology, historical manuscripts, and comparative religions as a guide (Bittanello, 2008; McColman, 2003). Celtic rituals practiced today are informed by knowledge of past techniques of communicating with the Otherworld. Examples include providing offerings of food, drinks, and art to the ancestral spirits, land spirits, and other deities.

The acts of daily life are often viewed as a form of ritual for modern pagans. Daily purification and protection rituals are performed and accompanied by traditional prayer and songs from sources such as the Scottish Gaelic *Carmina Gadelica* or manuscript collections of ancient Irish or Welsh poetry. Modern pagans also utilize traditional Celtic activities such as taking omens from the shapes of clouds or observing the behavior of birds and animals (Laurie et al., 2005). These mystical practices form a balance with scholarship to recreate Celtic religious practices as a living faith.

Those who follow the ancient religion today strive to follow and revive the religious and ritual practices of the Celts as faithfully and accurately as possible. However, they also acknowledge that some aspects of their spiritual practices may be inventions based on theories about the past (Littlefield, 2005). To ensure that they practice the religion as faithfully as possible, pagans often seek feedback from scholars to assess whether any new practice is acceptable or not.

One use of traditional Gaelic blessings for focus and intention-setting is to practice the morning ritual. This practice recognizes that every day is sacred in a unique way. The Celts believed this, so they greeted the sun at sunrise each day.

If you want to practice this ritual in your daily life, you should ideally face the sun at the moment of sunrise. If this is not possible, take a few minutes in the morning when you can. At this moment, greet the new day and send peace to the four corners of the world. Through this process, you recognize the uniqueness of the day you are about to experience, and you have the opportunity to embrace its energy.

Summary

This chapter has presented an overview of Celtic mythology, the important (and less-known) deities, and the origins of Celtic myth and legend, as well as a guide to Celtic rituals and how to incorporate them into your daily life.

The next chapter will explore another vital element of Celtic spirituality: Nature and landscape, which played a central role in Celtic religious practice to the extent that the Celts believed that the elements *were* gods.

Chapter Two

Nature and Landscape

I will arise and go now, and go to Innisfree,
And a small cabin build there,
of clay and wattles made;
Nine bean-rows will I have there,
a hive for the honey-bee,
And live alone in the bee-loud glade.
                    –W.B. Yeats, from "The Lake Isle of Innisfree"

WHAT CAN WE LEARN from the Celts concerning their attitude to nature and society?

The people of this ancient culture were famously one with the environment. They believed that all living things possessed a spirit. It is even the case that some of their gods were natural phenomena rather than human in form.

Celtic society was essentially rural, and everything its members did and owned was related to the land, the elements, and what these gave them.

So, good harvests were vital to the Celts' well-being.

Today, however, we are disconnected from our surrounding world. At present, around 4.4 billion people, or 56% of the world's inhabitants, live in cities. This figure will almost certainly increase, as shown with the estimation that, by 2050, it is anticipated that nearly 70% of the world's population will live in cities (The World Bank, 2023). This means that most people lack a connection with nature in its rawest form.

Due to the damage we have inflicted on our environment and how this has affected human health, there needs to be a change. So, below, we will explore the Celts' relationship with nature and landscape and consider how we can apply this ancient knowledge to our modern lives.

The Celts and Nature

The Celts had a deep connection to the landscape and animals. This connection played a significant role in their spiritual practices. They believed certain places were sacred and possessed powerful spiritual energy.

Additionally, as stated in the introduction of this book, the Celts were believers in animism. This is the idea that all things in the living world have a spirit or a soul. So, everything from humans and animals to plants, rivers, and rocks, all have an associated spirit. Notably, the Celts believed that animals were spiritual guides and messengers. Certain mammals like the stag and the boar had special significance to them and were often depicted in Celtic art and stories (Asher, 2023).

Many other natural features also had spiritual significance to the Celts, as you will find out below.

The Landscape and Its Features

Like many pre-industrial, Indo-European societies, the Celts believed that all parts of nature had spirits. This meant that every spring, river, lake, grove, or mountain was alive and had a deity associated with it. For example, the center of the Druidic stronghold on Anglesey was a sacred grove, as denoted by the Celtic *nemeton,* which was frequently used to allude to such areas (Green, 2011). This word was used to demonstrate the holiness of trees and forests.

Trees

The Celts believed that trees were the roots of spiritual life on Earth. Strabo, a contemporary of Julius Caesar, recorded that the Druids believed in the immortality of the soul that had been conceived and empowered by an indestructible universal divinity. The dryads, or tree spirits, associated with the sacred trees of the Druids, represented the spiritual ethos or nature of their one great creator, Celi—an invisible god whose very name means "concealing." Celi and his consort, Ceridwen, were believed to have been two "incomprehensible spirits" who dwelt beyond Earth (Paterson, 1997).

According to Druidic belief, the dryads had come to Earth through the first rays of the sun long before mankind appeared on land. Each sacred tree of the Druids therefore represented a cosmic symbol of primeval archetypal spirits, which later became associated with Celtic gods and goddesses who represented human archetypes (Paterson, 1997).

The Celts had a deep affinity with trees, believing them to be living beings with unique spiritual attributes. They also believed that these natural objects were a bridge between the earthly and spiritual realms. In particular, the oak was revered in Celtic culture. As the "King of Trees," it was associated with strength, wisdom, and the power of the Druids. Sacred groves were a common place for rituals, as the oak trees often found there were perfectly situated to act as altars (Asher 2023).

The significance afforded to trees in Celtic culture is reflected in the ogham alphabet. This was an ancient alphabet mainly used to write in the early Irish language. Around the sixth century A.D., it was used in the Gaelic kingdom of Dál Riada, located in modern-day Argyll, West Lochaber, and the Inner Hebrides of Scotland and the northern tip of Ireland. Ogham is known as the "Gaelic tree alphabet" or the "Celtic tree alphabet" because each letter is assigned a tree or plant name (Asher, 2024). This letter system is indicative of how fundamental nature was in Celtic cultural discourse.

Water

Water in all forms was venerated and seen as sacred in the Celtic world because it was viewed as a life source and a means of cleansing (Green, 1989). Abundant archaeological evidence survives of offerings of votive objects to the spirits of lakes, rivers, and bogs. One example is the discovery of rich aristocratic Celtic metalwork that had been cast into Llyn Cerrig Bach on Anglesey over the course of more than two centuries. This activity may have been associated with the existence of the Druids' sacred site on the island (Lynch, 1970).

Some experts have suggested that certain waters were considered so sacred that human sacrifices were made in them. For example, the remains of a young man who lived in the first century A.D. have been discovered in a marsh in Lindow Moss in Cheshire. The wounds found on his body suggest that he was likely a Celtic human sacrifice, perhaps made to appease the god of the bog. Traces of mistletoe were found in his stomach, which seem to have been part of a ritual that took place shortly before his death. This may indicate Druidic involvement in his demise, and it may have been the case that he was a Druid himself (Stead et al., 1986).

In contrast to the above instance, water was more frequently used for healing purposes. The Celts believed that pure spring water could heal disease. They also knew of the mineral and curative qualities of some waters, and they recognized and revered them because they provided the means for both physical and spiritual purification (Green, 1989).

The spiritual qualities of water are discernible by the cyclical understanding of it in the Celtic consciousness. As the Celts saw it, water fell from the sky as rain and was perceived as the gift of the sky god, and it was then absorbed by the earth and emerged as springs. This process highlights the links between the upper and the lower worlds as understood by this ancient culture (Green, 1989).

The main focus of Celtic water-cult practices during the Romano-Celtic period was springs, although some evidence exists that suggests that these sites had been venerated before the Roman period. It has been proposed that Gaulish springs were likely venerated in the Neolithic and Bronze Ages, while some spring sites such as Duchcov in the Czech Republic date back to the very early Iron Age. The end of the Celtic era and the onset of the Romano-Celtic phase saw a dramatic increase in religious practices around sacred curative springs (Green, 1989).

During the Romano-Celtic period, substantial shrines were established, and a large number of pilgrims visited them. One example is the cult of Sulis Minerva at Bath, which was based around the natural hot springs there. Sulis Minerva was a healer and goddess of retribution who was worshipped at a magnificent bath complex in the town. The Roman baths were created in the years between 60 and 70 A.D., after Boudicca's revolt. They were funded by Rome and organized by the army present in the area. Their creation is reflective of Roman technological skill and Gallic workmanship (Irby-Massie, 1999).

However, the springs at Bath had been of interest even before the Roman period. Celtic coins dating to the early first century A.D. had been recovered from the King's Bath Spring, while the name "Sulis" itself is etymologically related to the Suleviae, a Celtic triad originally worshipped in Germany as goddesses of fertility, prosperity, water, and healing (Irby-Massie, 1999). These examples indicate that the Romans exploited an existing Celtic religious and practical interest in the natural properties of water.

Nature as a Healer

The Celts also used nature to treat their problems and ailments. To this end, plants were used in religious rituals and consumed for healing. In his *Natural History XXIV*, Pliny records that: "The Druids of Gaul have recorded that it [the *Selago* plant] should be kept on the person to ward off all fatalities and that the smoke of it is good for all diseases of the eyes" (Green, 1997: 46).

The *Selago* plant was not just seen as medicinal by the Celts: It was also viewed as magical. Earlier in this passage, Pliny discusses the strange manner in which it had to be collected: "It is gathered without iron, with the right hand thrust under the tunic through the left arm-hole as though the gatherer were thieving" (Green, 1997: 46).

Mistletoe was also used for magical and medicinal purposes. It was used in rituals and also given to sick persons in a drink. It was believed to be an antidote to all poisons and to be an effective infertility treatment (Green, 1997). Pliny's text thus explains how magic and medicine were practiced together through the use of sacred plants.

The Elements

The Celts also acknowledged the power of the four core elements that made up life: Earth, Air, Fire, and Water. McCoy (1995) describes what the Celts connected with each of the four elements and why:

Water

Water, perceived as feminine, is the realm of the psychic and the dream world. It is the element of children, pregnancy, childbirth, purification, inner transformation, emotional healing, romantic love, manifestation, and death and rebirth.

It is commonly associated with items such as cups, cauldrons, drinking vessels, water, and wine. The element is also related to the season of fall and the westerly direction.

Earth

For the Celts, Earth, another feminine element, was the realm of stability and growth, and it was the home of the eternal Mother Goddess. It relates to prosperity, fertility, planting, harvesting, the home, and animals.

It was associated with items such as stone, clay, salt, gems, plants, weapons, and jewelry. Earth was the element of winter because the coldest winds come from the north, the direction Earth is associated with. This may be why north is the direction of orientation for maps.

Air

The air (masculine) is associated with the mind, which is considered to be an unpredictable realm in Celtic mythology and tradition. Consequently, the element relates to intellect, study, travel, and communication.

It is associated with objects like the staff, wand, sword, feather, incense, some weapons, musical instruments, and jewelry. It is also associated with spring because it brings new inspiration with it. East is its associated direction.

Fire

Fire, another element that is associated with masculinity, is the domain of passion and transformation. It relates to protection, exorcism, banishing, sex, work, purification, and masculine power.

Fire is associated with items such as candles, bonfires, wands, flint, ashes, torches, and gold. It is related to the summer season because it is the lightest, hottest time of year, and it is connected to the direction of the south.

Spirit

McCoy (1995) also observes that the Celts acknowledged the existence of a fifth element, Spirit, which was seen as a unifying force that animates all of the other elements. It was often represented in Celtic tradition by a cord.

The Festive Calendar

The Celtic festival calendar centered around celebrating the seasons and what each one and the natural changes it brought with it represented for the community. The four great Celtic festivals were Imbolc (February 1), Beltane (May 1), Lughnasadh (August 1), and Samhain (November 1).

Archaeological evidence suggests that the great Irish Celtic seasonal festivals were celebrated in similar ways at the same times of the year across the Celtic world.

In Coligny, Central France, archaeologists have discovered a fragmentary Gaulish bronze tablet dating to the first century B.C.E. Etched upon it is a timetable of religious festivals and cult events.

Notably, the word *samonios* is found on the tablet, which correlates with Samhain. The first fruit festival is entered on the calendar, indicated by the word *rivros,* and it takes place on August 1. This festival may be similar to Lughanasadh, which was held around the same time (Green, 1997). The Coligny Calendar is therefore evidence that proves that the seasonal festivals were universally celebrated across the Celtic world.

While the Celts celebrated the four midpoints between the four solstices and equinoxes, other ancient pagan peoples, such as the Anglo-Saxons mainly celebrated the four solstices and equinoxes (Hutton, 1993). This means that modern pagans tend to celebrate several festivals that were not universally celebrated by our pagan ancestors.

The eight festivals that make up the seasons of the year, including the solstices and equinoxes are as follows:

- Winter solstice (Midwinter/Yule)

- Imbolc (Candlemas)

- Spring equinox (Ostara)

- Beltane (May Eve)

- Summer solstice (Midsummer/Litha)

- Lughnasadh (Lammas)

- Autumn equinox (Mabon)

- Samhain (All Hallows)

A discussion of four of these festivals, namely Imbolc, Beltane, Lughnasadh, and Samhain, can be found in Chapter 1.

The Winter Solstice

From the late Stone Age onward, midwinter, or yule, has been recognized as a significant turning point in the year. It is commonly marked around December 21 because the day is generally the shortest of the year. The significance of the occasion is demonstrated by the existence of ancient megalithic sites at Stonehenge and Newgrange. At both locations, the sites are carefully aligned with the position of the sunrise and sunset at this time of year (Johnson, 2008).

The winter solstice marks the reversal of the sun's decreasing presence in the sky and symbolizes the rebirth of the solar god, a precursor to the return of the fertile seasons. In both Germanic and Roman traditions, this was an important cause for celebration.

The practices that occurred during the winter solstice varied between cultures but commonly involved sacrifices, feasting, and gift-giving. Also commonplace during this time was the tradition of bringing wreaths of evergreens like holly, ivy, yew, mistletoe, and pine into the home and decorating them (Zell-Ravenheart & Zell-Ravenheart, 2006). In Roman tradition, additional festivities also took place over the six days leading up to the midwinter festival.

The Spring Equinox

The spring equinox is the second of three spring celebrations practiced in paganism, and it is the midpoint between Imbolc and Beltane. During this time, light and darkness balance out once more, with the days getting increasingly lighter in the period that follows. As such, the spring equinox represents a time of new beginnings and the emergence of life following the sterility of winter.

In modern pagan traditions, the spring equinox is frequently called "Ostara." This word is a reconstruction by the linguist Jacob Grimm, and it comes from an Old High German form of the Old English word "Eostre." This is also the name of an Anglo-Saxon goddess of fertility for whom Bede says feasts were held in April (Sermon, 2022).

The Summer Solstice

The summer solstice marks the midpoint of summer and is celebrated on or around June 21, which is considered to be the point where the season reaches its height and the days last longest.

In modern Wiccan and pagan traditions, the festival is sometimes called

"Litha," which the Anglo-Saxon historian Bede (d. 735) recorded as the Saxon word for that annual point (Starza, 2023). Bede explained that the term means "gentle" or "navigable" because "in both these months [June and July] the calm breezes are gentle and they were wont to sail upon the smooth sea" (Beda, 1999: 54).

In some neo-Druidic traditions, the summer solstice is known as "Alban Hefin," the Druid name for that time of year, which translates to "the light of summer" in modern English (Starza, 2023).

The summer solstice celebrates the fact that the sun is at its greatest strength around this time of year. However, it also marks a turning point in the year, as at this point the sun also begins to decline, with daylight receding between June and December. The summer solstice is particularly revered among modern pagans and neo-Druidic groups due to its focus on the sun and the role of light as a source of divine inspiration. This event is often celebrated by modern pagans at Stonehenge.

The Autumn Equinox

Like the summer solstice, the autumn equinox has come to have far more significance to modern pagans than it did for our Celtic ancestors. This holiday is known to modern celebrators by a variety of names including Harvest Home, Mabon, Mean Fomhair, the Feast of the Ingathering, An Clabhsur, and Alban Elfed (to neo-Druids).

The autumn equinox is a neo-pagan festival that gives thanks for the fruits of the earth and recognizes the need to share them among the community to secure the blessings of the gods and goddesses during the winter months. Notably, one of its modern names, "Mabon" was invented around 1970 by Aidan Kelly, an influential figure in the Wiccan religion. The term refers to Mabon ap Modron, a character from Welsh mythology (Zell-Ravenheart & Zell-Ravenheart, 2006).

Religious beliefs changed over time. Most significantly, by the fifth century

A.D., most of Europe had been converted to Christianity (Green, 1997). However, this change did not mean the old festivals were abandoned entirely. Instead, these celebrations changed, evolved, and gained new meaning.

Imbolc evolved into Christian Candlemas and the folk legend Groundhog Day, which are celebrated as the modern holidays' ancient ancestor was on February 2. Meanwhile, Beltane was transformed into the great spring festival May Day, also known as Lady Day, which is held in honor of the Virgin Mary and celebrated on May 1. In turn, Lughnasadh evolved into the harvest festival, St. John's Day, and is celebrated on August 1 (Leslie & Gerace, 2000).

Perhaps the most interesting transformation of pagan festivals occurred around what was Samhain as it became the Christian celebration of All Saints' Day or All Souls' Day. This is also known as All Hallows' Day ("Hallow" is the Old English word for "Saint," as in "hallowed person"). Samhain evolved into a three-day festival with All Hallows' Eve (Halloween) celebrated on October 31, All Saints' Day on November 1, and All Souls' Day on November 2 (Leslie & Gerace, 2000). During these festivals, the idea of "the thin places" becomes relevant, as the divisions between this world and the Celtic Otherworld are particularly weak around this time of year, meaning that passing between the two is easier.

The old Celtic festivals are still celebrated today as part of the pagan revival. The eight core pagan festivals are celebrated by modern pagans as part of the Wheel of the Year, an annual cycle of seasonal festivals. These festivals, which are commemorated by many modern observers, mark the main solar events of the year, including all major solstices and equinoxes and the midpoints between them. The Wheel of the Year was created in the mid-20th century to mark these festivals, combining the four solar events, alternatively termed "quarter days," celebrated by many European communities, and the four seasonal festivals, or "cross-quarter days," that were celebrated by the Celts (Williams, 2013).

Celtic Festivals in the Current Era

Celebrating Celtic festivals is becoming increasingly popular. Many of these celebrations take the form of live gatherings, such as celebrations of Beltane at Butser Ancient Farm, in the county of Hampshire in the south of England, where a Wickerman is burned. A similar event is held at Circle Sanctuary Nature Preserve near Barneveld, Wisconsin. Beltane is celebrated in Edinburgh, Scotland, as a fire festival and carnival procession.

The close links between Celtic spirituality and the environment have made it particularly appealing to eco-spirituality. This is the case in expressions of both New Age spirituality and Christian spirituality. The Celtic religious tradition promoted a strong unity between all creatures and nature, as well as interdependence among the community. Even the most fearsome Irish chieftains practiced forgiveness toward their enemies and forgave exiles (Duncan, 2015). These features of the Celtic religious tradition are very attractive to modern campaigners for social justice.

Folklore and Fairies

Come away, O human child
To the waters and the wild
With a faery, hand in hand,
For the world's more full of weeping
than you can understand.

*—*W.B. Yeats, from "The Stolen Child"

Some Celtic folklore about the natural world tells tales of mythical or magical creatures. These stories abound and may have had their roots in the natural world.

The word "fairy" is believed to have either Celtic or Latin origins. "Faerie" comes from the Gaelic *fear shidhe*, meaning "man of the shee." Meanwhile "fairy" also derives from the Latin word *fatum* (Prabhat, 2011: 1).

In Celtic mythology, fairies are small, supernatural beings that have a human form but who can also fly. The first reference to their lore in the Celtic tradition appears in the writings of the learned elite, such as Giraldus Cambrensis (ca. 1146–1223). However, most of the fairy tradition was created in modern times, and they are frequently depicted in modern Celtic traditions. Like the fairies of other European traditions, those of Celtic origin are clever, mischievous, and capable of assisting or harassing humans (MacKillop, 2004).

On the other hand, the descriptor "fairy" has sometimes been used to describe characters that appear in Celtic folklore in a way that underplays the divine nature of these beings. In this sense, the idea of the fairy may have been an invention of later Christian writers and served as a means of making ancient Celtic tales less spiritual or religious.

Other magical creatures that appear in Celtic mythology include giants and kelpies. While giants and giantesses make appearances across Celtic mythology, they have little in common apart from their size. Irish and Cornish giants are often foolish and gentle while Scottish giants are generally more astute. Also, heroes are sometimes giants, with prominent examples including Fionn mac Comhaill and Cú Roí mac Dáire (MacKillop, 2004).

One prevalent example of giants in Irish mythology is the legend of the Giant's Causeway in County Antrim, located in Northern Ireland. The story goes that the Irish giant Finn McCool created a track to meet his rival, the Scottish giant Benandonner. After their meeting, Benandonner destroyed the causeway as he fled back to Scotland, creating what is seen at the site today (National Trust, 2024).

Another magical creature that makes appearances in Celtic folklore is the kelpie, a fairy water creature common in Scottish folklore. Kelpies were first thought to live in lonely, fast-moving streams. Later, they were believed to live in any body of water. Kelpies are usually depicted as horses and sometimes as humans. They are the least mischievous and most malevolent of the mythical creatures of Celtic legend. In the form of horses, kelpies are said to entice travelers onto their backs and then rush into deep pools of water to drown them. The creature's tail then strikes the water in thunder and, they disappear in a flash of lightning. As a human, the kelpie is a rough, shaggy man who leaps behind a solitary rider, whom it grips and crushes (MacKillop, 2004).

Sacred Sites and Journeys

The Celts had many sacred sites. These include stone circles, hill forts, and fairy mounds, all of which are discussed below.The Celts had many sacred sites. These include stone circles, hill forts, and fairy mounds, all of which are discussed below.The Celts had many sacred sites. These include stone circles, hill forts, and fairy mounds, all of which are discussed below.

Stone Circles and Standing Stones

Stone circles are to be found across the landscape of Brittany and the British Isles, and they have been dated to the megalithic period. They consist of standing stones arranged in rings. Experts estimate that they were built between 3300 and 900 B.C.E., with around 4,000 such monuments having been built in north-western Europe during this period. Around 1,300 stone circles survive today. Historians believe that the rest have been destroyed (Burl, 2000). Some noteworthy standing stones also survive, such as the Mên-an-Tol in Cornwall.

Many societies have erected stone circles throughout history. However, in the Late Neolithic and Early Bronze Ages, this particular tradition was limited to Britain, Ireland, and Brittany in north-western France. Significantly, the rings were not equally distributed across the regions. Most of them have been found in the Lake District, south-west England, the highland regions of Scotland, and south-west Ireland. Smaller groupings of stone circles can also be found in the Peak District, Wales, Wessex, the Wicklow Mountains, the Outer Hebrides, and Caithness (Burl, 2000).

The purpose for their origin has been lost to history. Archaeological investigations suggest that they may have had a ritual or ceremonial purpose, perhaps related to solar and/or lunar alignments. This is an assumption that can be made because, even today, festivals such as the summer solstice are hosted at Stonehenge around June 21 each year. Sometimes, stone circles were also used as cemeteries, with burials made in and around the main formation.

The most famous standing stones include Carnac in Brittany, Avebury and Stonehenge in England, Newgrange in the Republic of Ireland, and Calanais on the Isle of Lewis, Scotland.

Hill Forts

A hill fort is a type of earthwork that the Celts used as a defended settlement or a fortified refuge. They were located along mounds to create a defensive advantage for those defending the area. These retreats are a form of fortification that follow the contours of a hill; they have one or more lines of earthwork alongside defensive walls and external ditches.

Hill forts first appeared in the Late Bronze and Early Iron Age, and they were used by the Celts until the Roman conquest. In Britain, around 3,300 of them survive. Some examples can be found at Maiden Castle, Old Oswestry, Traprain Law, Hambledon Hill, Cadbury Castle, and Battlesbury Camp (Millgan, 2021).

Fairy Mounds

Fairy mounds are also known as fairy forts in English and *lios* or *raths* in Irish, which are words that mean "earthen mound." These are exclusively found in Ireland and are the remains of stone circles, hill forts, ringforts, or other circular prehistoric dwellings. Between the Late Iron Age and early Christian times, the Irish built circular structures with earth banks or ditches that sometimes had wooden buildings on top. As these dwellings were not designed to survive for a long period, vague circular marks are often all that is left of the ancient forts (Barber, 2014).

Fairy mounds are associated with local Irish traditions and folklore, often involving fairies and other supernatural entities who are said to defend these structures from destruction by farmers or builders (Magan, 2017). In 1991, 30,000 to 40,000 fairy forts were present in the Irish countryside, the oldest of which date back to as early as 600 B.C.E. (O'Giollain, 1991; Barber, 2014).

The mounds remain significant today, as they remind us of the Celts' strong bond with the land. However, while over 45,000 survive today, around 10,000 more have been destroyed since the first survey of them was made in the 19th century (Magan, 2017). This example shows how we often ignore and disregard our Celtic past.

Sacred Journeys

People have undertaken pilgrimages to Celtic religious sites since the time of the Celts, and they have continued into the Christian period, despite the purpose and significance of these sites having changed over that span.

Today, the original purpose of the Celtic sites has been acknowledged once more. Some examples include places like Stonehenge, hosting the summer solstice each year, and Glastonbury, having been reinvented as the site of a popular annual music festival. Other world-famous Celtic sacred sites include: Carnac in Brittany, France, Newgrange and the Hill of Tara in County Meath, Ireland, Skara Brae in the Orkney archipelago, Scotland, and Bryn Celli Ddu on the Isle of Anglesey, Wales, to name just a few.

One site of pilgrimage for the Celts was Avebury, which rivals the more famous Stonehenge in size, range, and atmosphere. For adherents of the ancient culture, Avebury had spiritual and ceremonial importance. It was built around 2500 B.C.E., and it is one of the world's largest stone circles. In this location, there are over 100 megalithic stones arranged in a large circle. The Avebury site includes the Sanctuary, which may have been connected to human sacrifice, and a burial chamber named West Kennet Long Barrow, which is one of the largest and most detailed still in existence. It was built around 3650 B.C.E. and was a place of festival, feasting, and ritual (Grace, 2022). The stone circle at Avebury and other buildings and features of the site indicate that the Celtic pilgrimage could be a varied and immersive experience.

One example of a Celtic religious site that later became a site for Christian pilgrimage and worship is Glastonbury, which is located in the south-west county of Somerset in the UK. The town is thought to have been a site of pre-Christian worship, perhaps because of the location of its famous Glastonbury Tor, the highest of the hills surrounding the town.

A form of terracing placed prominently around the tor was erected 4,000 to 5,000 years ago, which would have been the same time as Stonehenge (Johnson, 2024). These mysterious stones are said to have been remains of Avalon, meaning that, in the public consciousness, Glastonbury is often linked to the myth of King Arthur. Consequently, after England had converted to Christianity, Glastonbury, the small church on the Tor, and the abbey below it became sites for pilgrimage due to the legend that King Arthur and his wife, Guinevere, are buried in Glastonbury Abbey.

During the 1180s, having heard rumors about the presence of King Arthur's bones there, monks at the site's abbey decided to excavate the ground and discovered some small bones and some hair, which they claimed were accompanied by a stone slab. Underneath it, a lead cross was inscribed with the Latin version of "Here lies buried the renowned King Arthur in the Isle of Avalon" (Johnson, 2024). Historian Marc Morris (2008) suggests that the monks who "discovered" the remains were motivated by a need to increase the number of visitors to the abbey after it had burned down in 1184.

Nevertheless, the bones were placed in caskets and were later interred in a special black marble tomb in 1278 during a visit by King Edward I (Morris, 2008). This example shows how ancient Celtic spiritual sites were reinterpreted in the Christian era per traditional myths and legends about the early history of the British Isles.

Respect for Mother Earth

Celtic spirituality sees the divine in all the natural elements. In Celtic spirituality, everything is alive, pulsating with energy—trees have spirits, rocks possess wisdom, and water holds healing power. In this belief system, non-human entities are attributed to a spiritual essence. The Celts believed everything had a spirit—an idea known as animism, as we have explained. Nature was a teacher, guide, and healer to them.

To the Celts, every stone underfoot or gust of wind whispering through leaves was considered a manifestation of sacred energy. The Celts believed that each tree bore witness to life's mysteries, each river sang its own song of creation, and every creature held its unique piece of wisdom.

In our modern era, where disconnection from nature is common, such ideas may seem alien or fanciful. By recognizing our connection with the mysteries of nature, we enrich the quality of our everyday lives and find a deeper meaning and connection with all life. To foster your connection with this ancient tradition, and if you have the opportunity, visit local forests and bodies of water regularly. These places are where Celtic tradition dictates that spiritual energy is at its most powerful.

The intertwining trails of the ancient Celts as they roamed across Europe from their heartland in central Germany would eventually lead them to the emerald shores of Ireland. The verdant landscapes of the ancestral lands and their profound connection with nature became an intrinsic part of Celtic spirituality. It is one that paints a picture of life that is interconnected at every level. It speaks the language of trees whispering secrets to the wind, rivers singing lullabies to mountains, and stars telling tales to the night sky. It's like an ancient tapestry that has been woven with threads of wisdom drawn from earthy hues and celestial colors.

The Celts' appreciation of nature was not merely about reverence but also about learning from Mother Nature herself. Their relationship with the surrounding world was a two-way street. They respected and revered her, but they also learned from her and looked at the world around them to understand their place in it. The changing seasons taught them about the cycles of life and death, the perennial trees became symbols of resilience, and running rivers embodied the essence of moving forward.

We can learn from the ancient Celts to address our modern anxieties by seeking tranquility through nature. We can visit places of retreat and restoration for the mind and soul. At the very least, we can try to go outdoors every day, to an urban park or our own garden. However, we must be cautious not to treat nature with a consumerist attitude, and to use it for our therapeutic benefit alone, but deliberately to cultivate a relationship of *giving back* to nature, too. It is time to recognize and actively strengthen our connection to Mother Earth. It is crucial that we each do our part to stop harming our planet, take responsibility for our individual choices, and learn how to live more sustainably.

There are many ways of engaging more actively with nature. According to our circumstances, interests and locations, some of the following ideas could act as a springboard to get started: Mindful walking, forest bathing

(Shinrin Yoku), wild swimming (with due care), drawing in nature, meditating outdoors, volunteering for a tree planting and/or litter picking project, gardening (either in our own garden or an urban community garden), visiting sacred sites and undertaking a pilgrimage on foot.

Summary

This chapter has explored the spiritual significance of nature and landscape to the Celts. It is clear that nature was considered to be of prime importance in their world, and they fostered a strong connection to it, which has been lost in modern times. If we pay attention to their practices and incorporate some of these into our own lives, this connection can hopefully be rediscovered.

Connected to nature, but worthy of special attention, the next chapter looks at the significant role of animals in Celtic spirituality.

Chapter Three

The Animal Kingdom

Bird of the wilderness,
Blithesome and cumberless,
Sweet be thy matin o'er moorland and lea!
Emblem of happiness,
Blest is thy dwelling-place-
O to abide in the desert with thee!

–James Hogg, from "The Skylark Poem"

THE SACREDNESS OF NATURE and all natural phenomena led to profound respect and veneration of animals. Both wild and domesticated species became the subject of elaborate rituals and formed the basis of religious beliefs and practices (Green, 1992). This chapter explores how animals played a significant role in the lives and belief systems of the Celts.

Below, we will look at the role animals play in Celtic spirituality, mythology, and folklore and the kinds of symbolism attached to them. Then we will look at the relevance of the importance attached to animals in today's world, considering whether this is part of the Celts' legacy to us.

Animals in Celtic Spirituality

Like nature, animals played an integral role in Celtic spirituality due to the importance of the surrounding world to their way of life. Consequently, living creatures were valuable, as they sustained and assisted humans. They could be used for and provide food in the form of meat or milk, they helped humans in the hunt, and they could also contribute to human efforts in agriculture and warfare.

Unsurprisingly, animals also played an important role in Celtic spirituality. Davies (1999) remarks that the Celtic tradition is full of deities who take the form of mammals and birds. Many Celtic gods were depicted in semi-human, semi-animal form as a way of emphasizing the perceived close links between humans and the immediate environment.

One example is the archaeological discovery in Lezoux, France of a bronze head that takes the form of a bull-horned god. This item is believed to date to the first or second century A.D. (Green, 1997). The depiction of the gods as partially human and partially animal could suggest that practices that can be described as quasi-shamanistic formed part of religious practice in some parts of the early Celtic world.

Notably, the Continental Celts seem to have most admired the horned, stag-like god, Cernunnos. At present, over 30 representations of Cernunnos survive. "The Horned One" was the most important and perhaps even the principal god of this Celtic faction. He was a lord of nature, animals, fruit, grain, and prosperity, and he is portrayed as having a man's body and the horns of a stag. He is usually depicted in a squatting position and as wearing and carrying the sacred torc, an item of clothing often associated with this Celtic faction.

In addition to the renderings of Cernunnos, other proof of animal importance can be seen in it often being the case that depictions of part-human and part-animal figures show men or women dressed up as animals. Some evidence from early Ireland also suggests that the early bards wore a costume of bird feathers. Transmogrification, which is the transformation of humans into animals or vice versa, plays a significant role in the mythology of both Wales and Ireland (Davies, 1999).

The Celts attached sacred status to some animals, including dogs, horses, and ravens. Both the Continental and Insular Celts believed that the behavior of certain birds and land mammals could be interpreted and observed as omens. It has also been suggested that birds may have been seen as omens in pre-Christian Ireland (Davies, 1999).

As well as this, particular spirits had an affinity with certain animals. For example, the names of Epona, the equine goddess, and Artio, the ursine goddess, are associated with the Celtic words for "horse" and "bear," respectively (Green, 1997). Similarly, the Morrígan, an Irish goddess of war, is associated with wolves, ravens, crows, and horses; meanwhile, in Scotland, Brigid is associated with snakes and cattle.

The Celts also associated certain animals with particular mental or physical qualities and characteristics, as well as particular patterns of behavior. For example, animals like stags and horses were admired for their speed, beauty, and virility. Dogs were viewed as being good at hunting, having an excellent sense of smell, and being good at guarding and healing.

The physical qualities of animals could also be seen as being related to certain phenomena. For example, deer shed their antlers, so they were associated with cycles of growth (Wood, 2000). Meanwhile, snakes were seen as being symbolic of a long (or even eternal) life, as they could grow out of their skin and renew themselves; beavers, on the other hand, were believed to be skilled woodworkers.

These examples show how the Celts admired and acknowledged the real and perceived attributes of the animals they encountered. This then led them to revere or worship these qualities as a way of acquiring abilities they were lacking or only partially had (Green, 1998).

Animal Sacrifice

All over the Celtic world in shrines, graves, and settlements, archaeologists have found evidence of the regular sacrifice of animals, which served the purpose of satisfying the spirit world. It is important to note that this practice was not unique to the Celts, as it was widely practiced in ancient Greece and Rome as well as other parts of "barbarian" Europe (Green, 1997). Nevertheless, it was a practice of some significance, and it held economic value to Celtic communities. The slaughter of a cow, sheep, pig, or horse would have represented a serious economic loss for rural communities who might have been living and farming on the subsistence level.

The idea behind it was that the ritual of sacrifice transferred a life force to the Otherworld, which pleased the gods and established a channel of communication between the two worlds. The purpose behind the ritual-istic killing of animals may have been to give thanks and to appease certain deities. It may also have been a way of requesting good health and fertility or a means of seeing the future (Green, 1998).

Animals in Mythology and Folklore

Due to the significant role animals played in the daily lives of the ancient Celts, they are commonly portrayed in Celtic mythology. In these stories, myths, and legends, the tales of animals and birds are interwoven with those of humans and gods, and they explore themes important in Celtic society. This includes topics such as life and death, jealousy and lust, and love and hate. Some examples are explored below.

From the time of the earliest identifiable Celtic traditions at Hallstatt and La Tène, certain animals had specific associations in iconography and storytelling. It was common for shape-shifting gods and heroes to transform themselves into animals, while in Celtic Christianity, some saints such as Saint Pol of Brittany were thought to have power over living creatures. Meanwhile, others such as Saint Ailbe of Emly and Saint Ciwa were believed to have been suckled by animals (wolves) as was Bairre, an ancestor of the bard Amairgin (MacKillop, 1998).

Clues about the place of animals in Celtic mythology can sometimes be ascertained from stories recorded in the early Christian period. In the Christian era, the lives of the Irish saints sometimes contain accounts of animal sacrifice. For example, accounts of the life of Saint Patrick describe the gathering of princes, chiefs, or Druids at Tara to sacrifice victims to idols (MacCulloch, 1911).

Birds in Celtic Mythology

Birds are frequently mentioned in Celtic mythology as messengers between the worlds. Several Celtic myths describe mortals and divine figures who are transformed into birds for various reasons. This kind of transformation tends to be associated with ordeals, healing, shape-shifting, and journeys to the Otherworld (NicMhacha, 2005).

One type of bird often mentioned in Celtic myth is the blackbird. In the ancient Welsh tale "Branwen, Daughter of Llŷr," the god Brân the Blessed and his companions pass 72 years in a state of timeless enchantment as a precursor to the joys of the afterlife. During this time, they are serenaded by the birds of the goddess Rhiannon, which are blackbirds.

In another Welsh tale, "Culhwch and Olwen," blackbirds are described as "they that wake the dead and lull the living to sleep" (Byghan, 2020: 245). Also in this story, the hero is sent in search of the oldest animal in the world to ask it for advice concerning the location of Mabon, the god of youth or eternal life. Culhwch and his companions talk to five animals in turn, until they reach the oldest animal in the world. In order, these creatures are the blackbird, the stag, the owl, the eagle, and the salmon.

This myth casts the salmon as the oldest animal in the world, and the Celts associated it with wisdom. In the story, the salmon not only tells Culhwch and his followers where Mabon is but also gives them a ride on its back to the prison, allowing them to succeed in their quest (Trees for Life, 2023).

Other Examples of Animals in Celtic Myth and Folklore

Various other examples are mentioned by *Roman Britain* (2024), including:

The Badger

The Celts believed that the badger was fearless in the face of danger and was symbolic of courage and determination. For example, a badger acts as a guide during a dream in the Welsh myth of Pwyll Pen Annwn's courting of Rhiannon.

The Cat

In Celtic myths, cats are evil and ferocious. This may have been because felines were undomesticated in ancient times. Despite this, it was a potent totem animal and the representative of several clans. For example, Caithness was named after the clan of the Catti. Cats were also believed to be strong protectors, especially during warfare. For this reason, they were used as emblems in battle in the same way as geese, ravens, and boars were. One myth tells of Fionn mac Cumhail fighting with a clan of cat-headed people in Ireland. Perhaps this was a tribe that wore cat-skin helmets into battle?

The Cock

In many Celtic myths, the cock chases away ghosts and other monsters by crowing at dawn. For this reason, the Celts believed that the birds had the power to ward off negative forces.

The Crane

Many of the crane's attributes are shared with the heron. These include magic, shamanic travel, keeping and learning secrets, and discovering deeper mysteries and truths. Although, in the Celtic period, cranes were so common in the British Isles that one traditional belief that originated after the arrival of Christianity held that the birds are people who are paying penance for wrongdoing.

The Dragon

In Celtic mythology, the dragon can be depicted in various ways. It can take its standard form as a land-dwelling creature with legs, or it can be portrayed as a water serpent or a worm-shaped beast. This creature is usually presented as a benevolent dweller of caves, lakes, and inner Earth. Additionally, it is an ancient symbol of wealth. It also symbolized the power of the elements, especially Earth, and represented the contents of the subconscious mind. In terms of ritual, dragons often made appearances in initiation ceremonies.

They feature heavily in Celtic myths. There are several references to the Fianna fighting huge dragons in lakes. They were also believed to have been based at the sacred site of Kildare, where they lived under the protection of the goddess Brigid.

One notable myth that uses dragons as symbols of doom is that of King Arthur. Predictions of the future troubles with Arthur's kingdom take the form of dreams of dragons and serpents that occur at the time of Saint Mordred's conception. While King Arthur drives the beasts out, he is wounded. In his last dream, Arthur is finally devoured, which precedes his being killed in battle by his opponent, Mordred.

The Eel

The hero and demigod Cú Chulainn's spear, Gae-Bolga, was named after the eel (which is known as *eas-ganu* in Gaelic). In another instance involving this same mythological character, during a battle with Cú Chulainn, the Morrígan took the form of an eel to fight the hero.

The Fox

This creature symbolizes the ability to watch the motivations and movements of others while remaining unobserved. In Taliesin's "Song of His Origins," the Bard reports that he assumed the shape of a fox due to the animal's perceived cunning, slyness, and ability to make a fool out of those who chase it.

The Hawk

According to Celtic oral tradition, the oldest animal is the hawk of Achill Island. Like other birds, this bird of prey is a messenger between the world of the living and the Otherworld. What makes it unique is that it has greater skill and strength than any of the other birds, and it symbolizes clear-sightedness and good memory. If one is heard crying during a journey, this is a warning to be alert to a situation that requires boldness and decisiveness in its handling to avoid being thrown off balance.

The Mouse

The mouse is symbolic of secrets, shyness, cunning, and the ability to hide when in danger. If a mouse appears, it is a warning to pay attention to small details, such as the double meaning of words or the fine print of contracts. The rodent is frequently mentioned in Celtic folklore. For example, in a Welsh story about Manawydan and Pryderi, a mouse is depicted as the shape-shifted wife of the magician Llwyd.

The Otter

The Celts considered otters to be magical to a powerful extent. These creatures were believed to be strong protectors who could help others to gain wisdom and find inner talents; they also represent faithfulness and can recover from any crisis. In Celtic myth, during the voyages of Brendan, Maelduin, and others, the travelers were helped by otters.

The Pig

This animal is symbolic of the spiritual food that Druids consumed and that was served at festivals. Their meat was believed to be the magical, sacred provision of the Tuatha Dé Danann and swine were privileged by the sea god, Manannán mac Lir. They were also featured in *The Mabinogion*, when Pwyll, the king of Dyfed and husband of Rhiannon, was given pigs by the Otherworld god Arawn. Also, Merlin's writings say that he spoke with a little pig in his visions.

The Swan

This bird is connected with music and songs. It was also believed to help with the interpretation of dream transitions, symbols, and spiritual evolution. It also features in many Celtic myths and its feathers were used in the bards' ritual cloaks.

Animal Symbolism

Animal symbolism was an integral part of the Celtic religion, as demonstrated by what they represented in terms of battle and other phenomena such as the language of birds.

Beasts such as geese, ravens, and boars had strong associations with and were depicted as symbols of warfare. These creatures were linked to weapons and warriors because of their aggressive traits, which evoked imagery related to conflict and combat (Green, 1998).

Geese

The Celts saw geese as aggressive and alert, both appropriate qualities for war. Their bones have been found in the graves of Celtic warriors in Eastern Europe, and depictions of the birds were also commonplace on armor. This was the case with a rendering of a goose on top of the helmet of an Iron Age goddess found on a bronze figurine in Dinéault in Brittany (Green, 1998).

Ravens and Crows

Ravens and crows had an even stronger association with warfare in the Celtic imagination. These birds were viewed as cruel and representative of the carnage of war because they scavenge on dead flesh. The raven is prominently linked with carnage and destruction in the vernacular tales of Ireland.

Notably, the goddesses of war, the Morrígan and Badb, could change at a whim from human to raven form. As birds, they squawked dreadful omens and terrified armies with their presence. Significantly, the name "Badb Catha," attributed to one of the mentioned mythological figures, means "battle crow" in ancient Gaelic (Green, 1998).

One example of a depiction of a raven in relation to warfare is a third or second-century B.C.E helmet found in Ciumesti in Romania, which bears the figure of a raven on top. This archaeological discovery is especially interesting as the wings of the raven are hinged so that they would have flopped up and down in a realistic and unnerving fashion when the helmet's wearer ran toward an enemy (Green, 1998).

Boars

Boars had a special place in Celtic iconography from the earliest times (MacKillop, 1998). They were perhaps the animals that most significantly symbolized war in the Celtic imagination. This can be attributed to them being aggressively intimidating creatures that were strong, ferocious, and destructive. The Celts adopted the creatures as battle emblems, using them as motifs on weapons and armor, and they were supposed to protect warriors and ward off blows. They often appear on Iron Age sword stamps.

It is notable that nearly all war emblems of boars possess the feature of an exaggerated dorsal ridge that stands stiffly erect from the creature's back. This recalls the story of Diarmaid's foster brother, who is an enchanted boar and whose poisoned spines stand out like spikes. There is a stress on dorsal bristles in Iron Age art that expresses the ferocity of an angry boar and, thus, by implication, that of the warrior himself (Green, 1998).

The Language of Birds

Another form of animal symbolism that is commonplace in Celtic mythology is the language of birds, although it is not unique to this set of myths. It is also found in those of the Abrahamic and European religions, medieval literature, and occultism. It is a mystical, perfect divine language that birds use to communicate with the special few who understand it. All over the world, people believe that to learn the language of animals (particularly the language of birds) is to demonstrate an ability to discover the secrets of nature or "walk between the worlds" (NicMhacha, 2005: 47).

In ancient Indo-European religions, the behavior of birds was used to predict the future. Such customs may have begun in the Paleolithic period (early Ice Age) when humans looked for carrion by observing the movements of scavenging birds (Marzluff & Angell, 2007).

More specific to the Celts, according to early textual sources, the Druids could understand the language of birds. In Celtic tradition, the Druids are linked to the blackbird (known in Gaelic as d*ruid dubh* or "black Druid"). In ancient and modern Druidism, the blackbird is a messenger between our world and the Otherworld. To this end, an unnamed and uncredited ninth-century poem describes the blackbird's song as "a poem to the sun's first slender ray" (Byghan, 2020: 245; Carr-Gomm & Carr-Gomm 1994).

The relationship between humans and animals today remains as mutually beneficial as it was in Celtic times, although we do not value it as much as we should. According to the American Veterinary Medical Association (2024), the human-animal bond exists and is important to both human and animal health, as well as the health and welfare of the wider community.

Many modern families have at least one pet. The 2017–2018 National Pet Owners Survey, undertaken by the American Pet Products Association, found that 68% of households in the United States own at least one domestic animal, amounting to 84.6 million homes in the country. Dogs and cats are the most popular of these creatures in the United States, but other popular choices include horses, reptiles, birds, and fish (Michigan State University, 2018).

The importance of pets to modern people is further demonstrated by how animals interact with their owners every day, with many people treating their pets in the same way they treat other people. According to a survey completed by *The New York Times*, 70% of pet owners report sometimes sleeping with their pets, 65% buy their pets Christmas presents, 23% cook their pets special meals, and 40% of married women believe they get more emotional support from their pets than from their husbands (Michigan State University, 2018).

While surveys often center around what humans get out of their pets, it is apparent that animals also benefit from being around people. Namely, they need their owners to get their basic needs met. However, humans still receive the greater benefit from having pets. Research findings have shown that pets can reduce stress, lower blood pressure, raise oxytocin levels in the blood, and even reduce pain. Bayer (Michigan State University, 2018) has even found that living with dogs makes people 15% less likely to die from heart disease.

Other examples of the present-day human-animal bond include the growing call for a change in attitude toward more sustainable farming and animal husbandry, as demonstrated by the Compassion in World Farming organization. Another point that is worthy of mention is the growing popularity of veganism as a lifestyle, particularly among young people. For example, between 2014 and 2019, the number of vegans in the UK quadrupled from 150,000 (0.25% of the population) in 2014 to 600,000 (1.16% of the population) in 2019 (The Goodness Project, 2024).

Another example of evidence that we are beginning to renew our relationships with nonhuman living creatures is the popularity of trends such as "animal communication," wherein many hope to deepen their bond by understanding the secret language of the animal kingdom.

When it's put together, all this evidence suggests that the Celts were right to conclude that animals bring massive benefits to humans.

The Celts believed that humans could assume the attributes of animals. That is why the symbols depicting ravens, boars, geese, and even cats adorned the armor of warriors during warfare: Their wearers believed that these creatures' ferocious and fearsome attributes would somehow benefit the person that evoked them.

Today, we expect less from our nonhuman companions. However, like the Celts, we can learn from them. Good (2021) puts forward four key lessons we can learn from animals.

It is apparent that animals played a significant role in Celtic spiritual beliefs and customs as, like forces of nature, they were an integral part of the surrounding world.

The Celts valued and revered animals. Often, they used symbolism as a way of evoking the traits they believed certain animals possessed so that they could take on these attributes themselves.

Today, we do not always value animals as much as we should, yet studies prove that we benefit from regular contact with animals, and we can observe their behavior to learn to live better. Because of this, we should pay attention to how the Celts treated animals, as it can improve our lives for the better. Perhaps one way we can go about this is by implementing more sustainable farming.

This chapter has explored the role of animals in the Celtic tradition, and it has noted their relevance today. Moving on from this, the next chapter will look at the role of the Divine Feminine in Celtic tradition.

Chapter Four

The Divine Feminine in the Celtic Tradition

I am the fire upon the hearth,
I am the light of the good sun,
I am the heat that warms the earth,
Which else were colder than a stone.
At me the children warm their hands;
I am their light of love alive.
Without me cold the hearthstone stands,
Nor could the precious children thrive.

–Katharine Tynan from "Any Woman"

WOMEN HAD FAR MORE power in the Celtic world than their ancient Greek and Roman counterparts did. In Celtic societies, women had sexual freedom and could become political and spiritual leaders. However, women's influence waned after the Roman Conquest, as Rome was a

55

patriarchal society, and it imposed this view on its domains. It was a stance that was later promoted by the Christian religion.

In the Celtic world, women were also associated with divination, nature, and fertility to a significant extent. For these reasons, women in the Celtic world were seen as having divine and spiritual powers.

The Divine Feminine

The concept of the Divine Feminine is still widely discussed today. It refers to the energy that exists in and around us; it is all that is soft, nurturing, empowered, and intuitive. In other cultures, the concept has been interpreted as yin energy or Shakti, and it can be found in the moon, the trees, the ocean, and within us. In this sense, it is deeply connected to the natural world.

The Divine Feminine is who we are when we are allowed to be wild and untamed, and it remains with us when we are soft and still. It is the opposite of the Divine Masculine. When these two competing energies are in harmony, much like with yin and yang, we live in balance.

However, the problem with modern society is that it values masculine energy over feminine energy due to the dominance of a patriarchal order in the world system. This has lasted for millennia. Because of this prevalence, our society increasingly emphasizes the importance of masculine values and structures, so we often find ourselves disconnected from feminine energy. This shuts down the Divine Feminine. It also leads to the disempowerment of women in society.

If we can lean back into that Divine Feminine energy, we can achieve the light and balance we need to feel whole once more. By considering the significance of the concept in the Celtic world, we can do just that. This chapter thus first explores the position of women in ancient Europe before considering the role of the Divine Feminine in the Celtic world and its influence on modern traditions.

Position of Women in Celtic Europe

Historians do not agree about the position of women in the Celtic world. Some believe that women enjoyed a prominent position in society and full equality with men while others believe that they had something approaching mere equality with men (Watts, 2005).

The view that women enjoyed a standing equal to men is supported by the existence of female leaders, such as Boudica, and anthropological arguments. The Celts were a non-patrilineal society. In such systems, men marry women who are around the same age as them, whereas, in patrilineal systems, there is a much greater age gap between male and female partners. Although men were hunters, because it was women who sowed and harvested crops, they had high prestige in societies compared to those where men alone provided the food (Watts, 2005).

Furthermore, evidence from religious practice suggests that important positions were held by goddesses in the Celtic belief system, which may have been reflective of the importance of women in their communities However, societies where women were inferior to men, like ancient Greece, also had both male and female deities (Watts, 2005).

What is particularly notable is that Celtic women were allowed more than one sexual partner, and they had more freedom over their sexuality than was the case in other ancient societies. Julius Caesar reported this fact, explaining that (Watts, 2005: 14):

> Groups of ten or twelve men have wives together in common, particularly brothers along with brothers, and fathers with sons; but the children born of these unions are considered to belong to the particular home to which the maiden was first conducted.

Dio confirms that women in Celtic society enjoyed sexual freedom, recalling a conversation he had with Julia Domna, mother of the emperor Caracalla and wife of the Caledonian chieftain Argentocoxus in the third century A.D. She told Dio that "we consort openly with the best men" (Watts, 2005:14).

On the other hand, while women had some freedoms in Celtic society, it may not be the case that they had entirely equal status to men. Notably, Caesar observes that husbands had the "power of life and death" over their wives and children. It may have also been the case that the position of Celtic women changed after the Roman conquest due to the influence of Roman law and culture, which saw the man as being the head of the household.

On balance, though, the testimony of Classical authors, archaeology, and myth all suggest that some high-ranking Celtic women enjoyed a power comparable to that of their male peers (Green, 1997).

Extremely powerful and influential women could and did exist in Celtic Europe between the fifth century B.C.E. and the first century A.D. There were not many such women, but they were accepted in their society in a way that women in similar positions would not have been in ancient Greece or Rome. For example, in Classical Athens in the fifth century B.C.E., women were not even granted citizenship, and their only contributions to public life were in the sphere of religious activity (Green, 1997).

By way of contrast, evidence for the existence of powerful, high-ranking women in Celtic society can be found in myth, archaeological remains, and Classical writings.

Women in Myth

Queen Medb of Connacht is a central figure in *The Ulster Cycle*. She is depicted as an independent ruler with an army and is described as being more important than her consort. Medb was said to have boasted that she "was never without one man being with [her] in the shadow of another" (Watts, 2005: 14). However, she is a mythological figure, not a historical one, and she is a goddess rather than a human queen.

Other examples of powerful goddesses include Badb, who was believed to be the one who would cause the end of the earth. There was also the Morrígan, who was thought to be able to predict who would win in battle and who hovered over battlefields as a crow or a raven (O'Hara, 2023). What is interesting, though, is that Queen Medb and other examples suggest that the idea of powerful women was widely accepted across Celtic society.

Evidence From Archaeological Findings

Graves dating to Iron Age Europe point to the presence of independent, high-ranking women, who may have well been dynastic rulers in their own right.

The Lady of Vix

One example is the burial site of the Lady of Vix. The archaeological remains are those of the grave of a 35-year-old woman who lived at the end of the sixth century B.C.E. in Vix, located in northern Burgundy, France. She was buried at the foot of a hill on which stood the stronghold of Mount Lassois, dating back to the Early Iron Age. She was laid in the grave with great ceremony, and the body was first carried to the tomb on a great four-wheeled bier. This was then dismantled and placed with the corpse in a wooden mortuary chamber under a massive earth mound (Green, 1997).

The Vix lady was interred with many luxurious grave goods, including jewelry and vessels. For example, she was laid to rest with an enormous bronze krater (wine-making vessel) which stood at 5 feet, 6 inches high. This object would have been manufactured in Corinth in Greece or Eturia in Italy and, despite its size, would have been transported across the Alps to northern Burgundy.

Due to the craftsmanship involved in making it and how it had been transported across Europe, the presence of the krater in the woman's tomb is indicative of her high rank. The vessel implies that she had strong links with the Mediterranean world, either because she was from there herself or because it was a gift to her from another ruler (Green, 1997). The evidence therefore suggests that the Lady of Vix is an example of an autonomous female ruler in the Celtic world.

This is not the only example of an Early Iron Age woman buried with elaborate rituals and luxurious grave goods. In the fourth century B.C.E., another lady was buried at Reinheim beside the Blies River in Germany. She had been buried with a set of gold ring-shaped jewelry, including a torc and armlets. The adornments suggest that she was either important enough to commission the accessories or that the members of her community believed her to have a high or divine status (Green, 1997).

All the jewelry pieces were intricately decorated with metalwork engravings, including images of a female figure with her hands folded on her stomach in the manner of a corpse. There were also great birds of prey perched on top of her head, which is indicative of the divine status of the woman. While this iconography may represent a goddess, it could also depict the lady herself.

Evidence From Classical Writings

Classical writers confirm that high-ranking, powerful women existed in pre-Roman Britain. Two such women, Boudica and Cartimandua, took center stage in British politics during the mid-first century A.D. Both women came face-to-face with the Roman government, although in extremely different circumstances.

Boudica

Boudica (ca. 30–60 A.D.) was a member of the Icena, an East Anglian tribe. The historians Tacitus and Cassius Dio wrote about her exploits in great detail. She was the widow of the Celtic king Prasutagus, who had entered into a reciprocal contract with the Roman emperor Nero. This meant that Prasutagus's kingdom remained intact in exchange for him keeping the peace and allowing his realm to act as a buffer state (Green, 1997).

After Prasutagus died, Boudica assumed power (illegally, according to the Romans). Roman financial officials reacted by confiscating Icenian assets and abusing Boudica and her two daughters. This caused the queen to become enraged and gather a huge force of British freedom fighters, including the Iceni's neighbors, the Trinovantēs, who had also had problems with the Romans.

Boudica and her army caused a great deal of destruction in a short space of time, nearly driving their opponents out of Britain, including by sacking three major Roman-occupied towns, namely Londinium, Camulodunum, and Verulamium. These correspond to modern-day London, Colchester, and St Albans, respectively (Green, 1997). However, the rabble army was quickly defeated by the Roman general Suetonius, and Boudica died, either by suicide or from illness, shortly afterward (Davies, 2008; Vandrei, 2018).

Cartimandua

Cartimandua was the first-century A.D. queen of the Brigantes, a Celtic people who lived in what is now northern England. She reigned as queen from around 43–69 A.D. Cartimandua came to power at the time of the Roman conquest of Britain and presided over a large group of tribes loyal to Rome.

The only Classical account of her reign comes from the works of Tacitus, which suggest she commanded great influence across Roman Britain. Tacitus described Cartimandua as being of "illustrious birth," so it is likely that she inherited her position rather than having acquired it through marriage (Pennington, 2003). She was married to Venutius, and both she and her husband were loyal to Rome. One recorded example of their allegiance describes how the British resistance leader Caratacus sought sanctuary with them after he was defeated by Ostorius Scapula in Wales in 51 A.D. However, Cartimandua sent him to the Romans in chains. Consequently, the Romans awarded her commitment with great wealth.

Her downfall came when she divorced Venutius to begin a relationship with his armor-bearer, Vellocatus. From that point on, she shared her throne and her bed with her lover. Tacitus attributes Cartimandua's behavior to lust (Watts, 2005). Venutius reacted by making war against her and her Roman protectors in 57 A.D. Cartimandua was able to withstand her former husband's first rebellion thanks to prompt support from Roman forces.

When Venutius rebelled again in 69 A.D., she was not so lucky. Tacitus writes that he took advantage of the political instability in Rome during the Year of the Four Emperors, staging another revolt with help from other nations. When Cartimandua appealed to the Romans, they could only send her auxiliaries. She was eventually evacuated, leaving Venutius in control of her kingdom, which was now at war with Rome. After her defeat, Cartimandua disappears from the Classical sources.

It is important to note that female rulers such as Boudica and Cartimandua were exceptions to the rule in the Celtic world, as kings or tribal leaders were generally male. The implications of this are demonstrated by how, in his *Annals,* Tacitus observes that Cartimandua's rule was mocked by the Brigantes' neighbors, who "goaded" her people for "the shame of being yoked under a woman." (Armitage, 2020: 101).

The Divine Feminine in the Celtic World

The Divine Feminine is neither a simple concept nor a fixed entity. It is an ongoing dance of creation, destruction, and regeneration, mirroring the cycles we see in nature, from changing seasons to phases of the moon. When we understand this fundamental aspect of Celtic spirituality, our own lives can become more balanced and meaningful.

Notably, the Celtic understanding of the Divine Feminine perceived divinity not as distant and abstract but as intimately intertwined with everyday life. For that reason, some of the most powerful examples of the concept in the Celtic world relate to women completing everyday tasks that highlighted their value to the communities they lived in and the goddesses that represented the three stages of the female life cycle: The maiden, mother, and crone, each of which had a unique value in the Celtic world.

The Divine Feminine and its significance in the Celtic world can be understood by outlining the spiritual function of Celtic women in their communities and also by considering examples in the myths that survive about Celtic goddesses.

Celtic Women and Spiritual Power

The Divine Feminine was expressed in Celtic society by an appreciation of women as having a special connection to the spirit world. For this reason, they were often associated with the power of divination and the ability to cast magic.

Divination

Women had a strong association with prophecy and other magical powers in the ancient world. It appears that the Celts believed that women were uniquely gifted with the power to see events yet to unfold. Caesar, Strabo, and Tacitus all speak of the presence of Germanic priestesses whose principal function was divinatory, with their predictions often being associated with war (Green, 1997).

Tacitus refers to a belief among the German tribes that women were particularly blessed with such powers. He explained that the most powerful such woman was Veleda, who enjoyed divine status and was her tribe's political negotiator. In his *Histories, Book IV* the historian recalls (Green, 1997: 97):

> But any approach to Veleda or speech with her was forbidden. This refusal to permit the envoys to see her was intended to enhance the aura of veneration that surrounded the prophetess. She remained immured in a high tower, one of her relatives being deputised to transmit questions and answers as if he were mediating between a god and his worshippers.

Veleda was not the only woman in Celtic Germany known for her powers of divination. Julius Caesar also told of how, in certain Germanic communities, women had the responsibility of deciding, through divination, whether or not to wage war. This practice may have been commonplace in other parts of the Celtic world. This is supported by an instance in *The Ulster Cycle* when the Druids at the court of Queen Medb prevent her from engaging in battle when the omens are unfavorable (Green, 1997).

Witchcraft and Magic

There are surviving accounts of Celtic women performing magic, with archaeological evidence demonstrating how women had been organized into magical covens and guilds. The findings further indicate that the belief in their powers was real and taken seriously.

One example is in the form of an inscription that was discovered in a tomb in Larzac, located in southern France, in 1983. An inscribed lead sheet was found on a tablet that had broken into two pieces and which covered a pot containing the remains of a woman. On its four sides were 160 words in Gaulish that had been written using a Latin script. This amounts to an account of the presence of two rival groups of female magicians ("women endowed with magic"), and the text describes how one group had attempted to harm the other through magical means. The wronged magicians then employed wise women to neutralize the evil charm (Green, 1997).

Archaeological remains also point to a belief in the existence of witches or women with magical powers in the Celtic world. The Romano-British cemetery at Lankhills, Winchester contained burials of several old women dating to the fourth century A.D. These women had been decapitated, and their heads were placed by their legs.

A similar pattern of ritual behavior has been found in other Celtic cemeteries that have been studied in Britain. A very specific and gruesome rite took place at Kimmeridge in Dorset, England in the late third century A.D. In this cemetery, the bodies of elderly women were decapitated and laid to rest with their lower jaws removed and their heads positioned by their feet. Each body was also accompanied by a spindle whorl (Green, 1997).

The practice of removing the head from the body and placing it by the legs was common in Celtic times, as it was a way of positioning the dead in the direction of the Otherworld. However, the removal of the lower jaw implies a desire to prevent the deceased person from speaking. Because of this, it may have been that these women were known to have cast spells in life and that the community was worried that they might continue to do this in death—unless they were explicitly prevented from doing so (Green, 1997).

The presence of spindle whorls in the graves of the Kimmeridge women is also significant as in the Classical and Celtic religions, the spindle is a symbol of fate and destiny. The Roman Fates and some Gaulish Mother

Goddesses were perceived to be able not only to predict the life and death of humans, but they were also perceived to be able to end life by snapping the thread of their spindles. The presence of these objects in the graves may therefore suggest that the ladies were believed to also possess this ability (Green, 1997).

Goddess Worship

Across time and place, the concept of the Divine Feminine has been personified in the form of a great mother goddess. This figure is the embodiment of all things and brings peace and order to the universe. As such, the Divine Feminine was revered in Celtic spirituality partly through goddess worship.

The concept's significance to the Celts is demonstrated by the commonplace nature of exalting female deities in the Celtic world. These beings were widely venerated due to the association of women with fruitfulness and the importance of fertility for nature and agriculture to flourish. Archaeological evidence suggests that the Celts worshipped a mother-goddess-like figure who was an embodiment of the land. She was also the "most widely known female deity" among the Celts (McCoppin, 2023: 21).

The name of the mother goddess appeared in many forms in various Celtic cultures. The name "Danu" is most common in Ireland. Evidence suggests that Danu was one of the most ancient Celtic deities and that the name means "wisdom" or "teacher." As mother goddess, Danu was conceived by Earth itself. Today, two hills in a valley west of Killarney in County Kerry, Ireland, are still identified as "Dá Chích Anann" or "the Paps [breasts] of Danu" (McCoppin, 2023). She is also closely associated with fertility.

Archaeological findings and myths demonstrate that the Celts often associated aspects of the natural world with deities. In particular, there was a strong association between divine female figures and water in the Celtic world. Some examples include Sequana, the goddess of the Seine in France, and Boann, the goddess of the River Boyne in Ireland.

Many Celtic goddesses were also linked to the fertility of nature, as demonstrated by the many artistic renderings of fertility goddesses that survive, such as the *sheela na gigs*, which are carvings that show a woman displaying her vulva (McCoppin, 2023).

The importance of female goddesses and their power is illustrated by the existence of the process known as the "sacred marriage." It was said that for Celtic kings to receive their status, a fertility goddess who had a direct connection to the prosperity of the land needed to sanctify the coronation. This process required a sexual encounter between the king and a priestess, who played the role of the fertility goddess so that the new ruler could serve as the figurehead for the virility of the land (McCoppin, 2023).

The Goddess Brigid

One goddess that symbolized many aspects of the Divine Feminine was Brigid. She was the pre-Christian Irish goddess of fire, smithing, fertility, cattle, crops, and poetry (MacKillop, 1998). She is the most powerful female religious figure in Irish history. At various times, she has been a triple goddess, a virgin mother, a lawmaker, a virgin saint, and she has been a folk hero (Condren, 1989).

In Celtic mythology, Brigid is often associated with the goddesses of other cultures, such as the Greek Aphrodite or the Roman Minerva. She also has a strong connection with the Divine Feminine as, in many ways, she is the archetype of the "good female" principle, to the extent that she is compassionate, nurturing, and loving (Condren, 1989; Berg, 2022).

Early Irish sagas that include Brigid depict her as a beloved figure who embodies many aspects of the Divine Feminine. She is commonly presented as a healer, poetess, and smith-worker—roles that encompass nurturing care, creative inspiration, and transformative power. Brigid's example reveals how deeply entwined spiritual vitality was with practical activities for early Celts. This is further exemplified as she occupied both hearthside and cosmic realms.

Brigid is also a force for transformation and of womanhood itself. She embodies the qualities of both the maiden and the crone. As a young woman, she was known for her beauty. In her later years, she became a wise and sage-like figure. Significantly, the Triple Goddess, who Brigid is closely associated with, represents the three stages of womanhood: maiden, mother, and crone. As she embodies all these stages, she is a powerful figure in Celtic spirituality (Berg, 2022).

Brigid's connection to the Divine Feminine makes her a powerful role model for women today. In a world that tends to value power and success over empathy and compassion, the example of this deity reminds us of the importance of feminine power. She shows us that it is possible to be kind and loving while remaining strong and powerful.

Furthermore, it is important to remember that the force of the Divine Feminine is not solely a Celtic concept. Dr. Malgorzata Oleszkiewicz-Peralba (2009) observes that there are significant parallels between various global cultures' perceptions of Divine Feminine characteristics, a point that highlights the universal relevance of these figures, even today.

Spiritual Warriorship

Classical writers observed that female leaders were commonplace in Celtic Britain. For example, in his *Agricola XVI,* Roman historian and politician Tacitus (ca. 56–ca. 120 A.D.) writes: "for the Britons make no distinction of sex in their leaders." Furthermore, in his *Annals XVI* 34, the same writer quotes a British contemporary who told him: "We British are used to women commanders in war" (Green, 1997: 94). Two prominent examples, Boudica and Cartimandua, have both been discussed in this chapter.

Female deities such as Medb, the Queen of Connacht, and the Morrígan are also often presented as examples of women warriors. Both these goddesses have a prominent connection with war and power, so they also function as examples of the importance of feminine dominance in the Celtic world.

Women and the Hunt

The Celts did not see warlike qualities as being entirely alien to women, as demonstrated by the many depictions of hunting goddesses that have survived. Such images were often associated with battle imagery. One example is the iconography on a model bronze wagon discovered in the seventh century B.C.E. cremation grave of a warrior at Strettweg in Austria. It depicts a ritual stag hunt, and a statuette of a divine woman is portrayed supporting a great cauldron in her upstretched hands (McCoppin, 2023).

Celtic goddesses may have been so revered because the hunt was "associated not just with the chase and with killing but also with nourishment and renewal" (Green, 1997: 1888). Artistic imagery of these deities supports this assertion, as they are shown presiding over aspects of birth, death, and renewal. The inclusion of a cauldron with the figure of the woman depicted on the Strettweg model wagon also shows that the Celts linked the hunt and fertility, as acquiring meat would nourish the community and renew it. Similarly, acts of war could also be associated with renewal, if they were successful, and they could bring the community prosperity.

Women Warriors

It has been proposed that female warriors played as much of an important part in Celtic society as their male counterparts. However, most of these women have been removed from myths and written histories due to the influence of the patriarchal cultures that succeeded the Celts, such as the Roman and Christian cultures and these sources recorded most of what we know about the Celts and their world (Mountain, 1998).

Despite this, examples of women warriors do appear in Irish Celtic mythology. Some examples are presented below:

- **Scáthach:** She was a female warrior who appeared in *The Ulster Cycle*. Her exploits take place in modern-day Scotland, where she tells the hero Cú Chulainn how to complete several quests. However, when he catches her with her guard down, he forces her to become his lover.

- **Aífe:** She is a rival to Scáthach and, like her, Cú Chulainn forces her at sword point to sleep with him. She then becomes pregnant and gives birth to his son.

- **Neasa:** Also known as Nessa, she was a woman warrior who was forced at sword point to marry the warrior Druid Cathbad. She then became mother to the famous hero Conchobar mac Nessa.

- **Liath Luachra:** She is briefly mentioned in *The Fenian Cycle* as a guardian to the young Fionn mac Cumhaill. In "The Boyhood Deeds of Fionn," she raises the boy alongside his aunt, the Druidess Bodhmall, after his father, Cumhall, is killed by Goll mac Morna. Together, they raise Fionn in secret in the forest of Sliabh Bladhma. They teach him how to survive on his own until his fame threatens to bring his father's killers to him. They then send him away for his safety (MacKillip, 1998). Beyond this, very little is known about Liath Luachra.

These four women are all portrayed similarly. While male warriors were the protagonists and heroes of ancient Irish mythology, their female counterparts tended to be quickly overpowered by male warriors and heroes, often obliged to become their lovers and bear their children. In this sense, the Christian scribes who recorded these myths ensured that these women conformed to the narrow feminine standards their society imposed on all women.

While male warriors were depicted as fighting for honor and glory, their female counterparts were introduced into these narratives to emphasize the skill, accomplishments, and sexual power of the male "hero," who demonstrates his power by "conquering" them (O'Sullivan, 2024).

The only female warrior who was not portrayed in this manner was Liath Luachra, who acted as a guardian to the young hero, Fionn mac Cumhaill. As Fionn was a child, the relationship between them was maternal rather than sexual. However, like all the other female warriors mentioned in Irish mythology, she is reduced to assisting the male hero rather than being presented as a powerful warrior figure and heroine in her own right.

Significance of Spiritual Warriorship Today

Today, spiritual warriorship does not necessitate going to war. Instead, to embrace the practice, the image of battle is transformed into a call to take action and is a means of overcoming fear and anxiety. In this sense, we can harness the power of the Divine Feminine to take control of our lives in ways that bring balance through utilizing our feminine power.

One of the greatest acts of courage for those who have been silenced is to speak up against injustice. There is also a need for a shift regarding what skills are valued in society—with the recognition that, to achieve conflict resolution, more status needs to be given to the traditionally feminine "soft skills" of listening and compassion. This is what being a warrior entails in modern life. It takes a brave soul to stand up for kindness and respect in our relationships with each other, with other nations, and with the planet.

Summary

This chapter explored the significance of the Divine Feminine in Celtic society by exploring the position of women in the world in general and then linking the relevant examples to the spiritual functions of Celtic women and spiritual warriorship.

Celtic women enjoyed far more power and freedom than their counterparts in ancient Greece and Rome. However, following the Roman conquest, many of these freedoms were lost, and the stories of women warriors were mainly erased because they threatened the Roman and, later, Christian patriarchal systems.

An understanding of the Divine Feminine was also present in Celtic society. Women were revered as having powers of divination, worshipped as goddesses, and even allowed to become warriors and leaders. In this sense, female power was understood and appreciated in the Celtic world. However, a similar understanding of the Divine Feminine is often lacking in modern society. By understanding how important the concept is to balance and well-being, we can embrace it once more.

From this, we move on to the final chapter, where we will consider why the Celts considered art to be sacred.

Chapter Five

The Arts as Sacred

We can make our minds so like still water that beings gather about us that they may see, it may be, their own images, and so live for a moment with a clearer, perhaps even with a fiercer life because of our quiet.

–W.B. Yeats, from *The Celtic Twilight: Faerie and Folklore*

THE ARTS ENJOYED AN elevated status in Celtic cultures, as demonstrated by the considerable cultural output. These societies are known to have loved music, singing, dancing, art, and poetry. However, they are most famed for their storytelling, some of which has survived into the present day, both through enduring tradition and because it was written down by Christian monks in the Middle Ages.

In this chapter, we explore each of these art forms in detail and consider their impact and purpose today.

Storytelling

Storytelling traditions in the Celtic world revolved around the spoken word. Tales of the real and imagined past would be told at the fireside to educate the community about their world and beliefs. In "Book VI" of his commentary on the Gallic Wars, Julius Caesar wrote an account of the behaviors of the Druids. One of his most interesting observations concerns how much value the Druids placed on memorizing stories (Green, 1997: 10):

> It is said that [the Druids] commit to memory immense amounts of poetry. And so some of them continue their studies for twenty years. They consider it improper to entrust their studies to writing ... I think they established this practice for two reasons, because they were unwilling, first, that their system of training should be ... [spread] among the common people, and second, that the student should rely on the written word and neglect the exercise of his memory.

Caesar's observations demonstrate the value placed on storytelling in Celtic culture. In Ireland at this time, the official *scéalaí*, or the "teller of tales," told tales to kings and nobles at the great assemblies and fairs held at Teltown or Carman.

The scéalaí had a large repertoire of tales, including narratives about the supernatural world based on ancient Celtic myth. In these mythological stories, the Tuatha Dé Danann ("People of the Goddess Danu") are the main Otherworld race. Many of the people in these tales are the Irish versions of Celtic divine beings (Lysaght, 1999).

The scéalaí would have also told tales from *The Ulster Cycle*, although they are less commonplace in Irish oral tradition. The most popular are those that tell of how Cú Chulainn (the "Hound of Chulainn") got his name and how he killed his son, Conlaí, in single combat after failing to recognize him. Nevertheless, stories from this body of myths were a prestigious part of the scéalaí's collection of stories.

Another name for the scéalaí was *seanchaí* (meaning "historians" or "storytellers"). These were those figures, or the *seanchas*, who taught others about the past. Their role was to know the tales, poems, and history required of their rank, which was low down in the hierarchy of Irish storytellers, and to tell these to entertain their chiefs and princes. They also had the job of guarding details of the ancestry of their community to preserve the memory of long-dead ancestors.

The Storyteller in Celtic Myth

Tales from Irish folklore provide insights into ancient storytelling beliefs. The reason why Celtic culture survived was because of its rich storytelling tradition. This is alluded to in an Irish chronicle called "The Táin" ("Táin Bó Cúailnge" or "Cattle Raid of Cooley"). This story tells of how all the great poets and storytellers of Ireland were once called together in a council by the chief poet of the island. They had all been summoned because it had been discovered that a particular story of a famous cattle raid was no longer intact. Separate parts of the story were known by different poets, but none could recall the full story (MacEowen, 2007).

The chief poet of Ireland, known as the *ollamh* (pronounced "o'lav") hoped that by gathering all the most learned bards of the land, they could get together and use their shared knowledge to complete the tale. However, they were unable to do this. The full story was not recovered until a young poet named Muirgen sat down at the graveside of a once-great hero named Fergus mac Róich. Muirgen offered a small praise poem to honor the man but then found himself immersed in a mist. In it was the spirit of Fergus mac Róich, who for three days and nights conveyed "The Táin" in its entirety to Muirgen (MacEowen, 2007).

Storytelling in the Present Day

This story demonstrates how Celtic spiritual knowledge survived and was transmitted from generation to generation. As we have lost our connection to a spiritual way of seeing and living, we have lost the sacred knowledge of the past. A lack of storytelling culture means we have let ancient knowledge and wisdom slip away.

It is solely down to the power of story that we have a lingering Celtic tradition at all, the importance of which is exemplified in the following quote: "Story is stitched to memory. Story is woven in breath. Story is laced with blood and bone. Story pulses within dream and vision" (MacEowen, 2007: 18).

Today, in Celtic enclaves around the world, it is still possible to hear the vibrant stories of brave chieftains, great feasts, warrior poets, battles, Druids, warrior queens, Otherworld voyages, and encounters with various spiritual beings.

Poetry and the Tradition of the Bard

For the Celts, poetry was an important means of passing ancient knowledge and stories from one generation to the next. Notably, Julius Caesar recalled how the Druids memorized a large amount of poetry and that some of them spent up to 20 years studying and learning Celtic myths and legends (Green, 1997).

While many of these ancient poems did not find their way into writing, one of the earliest surviving examples of Celtic poetry is a eulogy to Saint Columba (ca. 521–597 A.D.) by Dallán Forgaill, one of the chief poets of Ireland. It is written in rhetorical short sentences linked together by alliteration, a device also used in sagas. The poem contains examples of the oldest known meter, where the two half lines are linked by alliteration, a system often found in early Germanic verse (Greene et al., 2024). This example suggests that ancient Celtic poetry was likely carefully crafted and then memorized by successive generations of storytellers.

Because of the complex nature of poetic memory and storytelling, those who memorized and told these stories were highly esteemed. One kind of storyteller found in the Celtic world was the bard. This was a high-status poet who acted as the voice of a group of people or a nation.

The word "bard" was first used by Thomas Gray in his 1757 poem "The Bard" (MacKillop, 1998). The Oxford English Dictionary describes these figures as (Strabone, 2018: 82):

> An ancient Celtic order of minstrel-poets, whose primary function appears to have been to compose and sing (usually to the harp) verses celebrating the achievements of chiefs and warriors, and who committed to verse historical and traditional facts, religious precepts, laws, genealogies, etc.

However, the origins of the word are ancient, and it was around long before the 18th century. Bards (or *bardds*) existed in medieval Gaelic and Welsh societies and were professional poets, employed to compose poems and tributes for their lords. They expected to be paid well by the man they worked for. If he did not pay them enough, a bard might compose a satire (*fili* or *fáith*) to mock him with.

Bards did not exist in all Celtic societies. In other parts of the Indo-European world, the role was fulfilled by similar functionaries such as rhapsodes, skalds, scops, and minstrels. Some of these positions were hereditary in Proto-Indo-European societies, such as was the case in ancient India and medieval Ireland (West, 2007).

The bards sang songs that recalled the brave deeds of tribal warriors and also preserved memories of the genealogies and family histories of the ruling dynasties within Celtic societies. While the pre-Christian Celtic people had no written histories, they did maintain an intricate oral history that they committed to memory and that the bards transmitted to the wider community. These figures used poetic techniques such as rhyme and meter to remember details and make them memorable and interesting to their audience.

In Druidic tradition, the bard wore blue robes, which was their color, as it is the color of the sky, peace, tranquility, and love. It is the color of Heaven and of the sunshine and serenity it contains, and it signifies the role of the bard as a memorialist of what has come before him (Williams ab Ithel, 1874).

Thomas Gray's borrowing of the word "bard" owes itself to the Welsh tradition, as the role and status of the figure varied from one Celtic nation to another. Ancient Roman commentators reported that among the continental Celts, they were singers and poets who occupied a lower status than the *vates* (interpreters of sacrifice) or the Druids, who commanded the highest esteem (MacKillop, 1998).

In Ireland, the bard held a low rank among the seven orders of fili (poet). The highest rank was the ollam or *ollaimh*. To reach this status, they would have had to master 350 stories over 12 years of study. The other ranks were fili (poets), bards, and seanchaidh (historians or storytellers).

The power and position of the bard in Wales, on the other hand, came before and survived after the rank of the hereditary princes. Some of the earliest recorded Welsh bards date back to the sixth century A.D. and include the Aneirin, Taliesin, Blwchbardd, Cian, and Talhearn Tad Awen. Only the *pencerdd* (chief poet or musician), whose training lasted nine years, was allowed to teach a bard in Wales (MacKillop, 1998).

The early history of the bards is only known to us today through myths and legends. One of the earliest recorded mentions of the group appears in *The Book of Invasions,* an Irish collection of poems and narratives, in a story about the Tuatha Dé Danann who became the *aos sí* ("folk of the mound"), comparable to fairies in British tradition. During the 10th year of the reign of the last Belgic monarch, the Tuatha Dé Dannan invaded and settled in Ireland. Afterward, they were divided into three tribes. The tribe of Tuatha became the nobility, the Dé became the priests, and the tribe of Dannan became the bards. While the myth of the Tuatha Dé Dannan is legendary, this story became an integral part of the Irish bards' history of their profession.

According to Irish mythology, one of the most famous bards was Amairgin Glúnmar (the "big-kneed"), who was also a Druid and a judge for the Milesians. He is said to have introduced lyric poetry to Ireland when he compared himself to several powers of nature, such as the wind, the waves, and the bull, in a poem composed the moment he set foot in Ireland. In another recited poem, he compares himself to many things, including a salmon, a sword, a plant, and a spear. Consequently, several learned commentators have suggested that he may have been borrowed by Welsh storytellers as a model for Taliesin (MacKillop, 1998).

Although today bards and the tradition of Celtic poetry have experienced something of a resurrection, by the 16th century "bard" was a term of contempt in Scotland. For example, around the year 1500, the poet William Dunbar said "Bot wondir laith wer I to be ane baird," translating to "But I would loathe to be a bard" (Strabone, 2018: 82).

Despite the lowering of the bard's status over time, today the figure has experienced a revival. Respecting poetry and the Celtic tradition means following the bard's path and harnessing the power of words for personal growth through poetry, storytelling, or songwriting. A modern bard should be skilled in many kinds of communication, including writing and relaying mythology. They should also have a good grasp of history so that they can understand and recite the myths and legends of their nation or pagan tradition (Calefia, 2012).

The Spoken Word

Celtic poetry and storytelling have survived into the modern era through the spoken word tradition, which reinterprets the convention of fireside storytelling for contemporary audiences. While the practice thrived for centuries in Celtic lands, it experienced a period of decline following the invention of television and radio.

Recently, a new generation of poets, rappers, and spoken-word performers have emerged. They tell tales for and about modern Ireland, thereby creating a new oral tradition that has its origins in Celtic storytelling. These modern bards perform everywhere: on stage and television or in streets, clubs, and pubs. They even sometimes reach the kinds of audiences their ancestors could never have imagined.

The artistic director of the Project Arts Centre in Dublin, Cian O'Brien explains: "There's definitely a renaissance [in spoken word]. You can really see it around the city ... It's the younger generation trying to find a way to tell their stories in a way that makes sense to them and their audience" (Carroll, 2018: 1).

The spoken word is popular with contemporary crowds because it brings a different, extraordinary energy to performances. Also, through the spoken word, audiences can see themselves and experiences that reflect their lives depicted on stage.

How spoken word resonates with audiences today indicates how Irish poetry and oral tradition was spread through people gathering around to hear stories, suggesting that Celtic literary forms bring art back to its core foundation, which is a way to bring people together and unite the community.

The Written Word

Before the Roman Conquest, the Celtic world was virtually illiterate. This means that there is no written record of what took place before that time. The few pieces of linguistic material that do survive from the pre-Roman period of history consist of the names of places and people that are found in Classical literature and inscriptions. Some of the latter are single words, usually names, found on coins. Despite this, some quite long inscriptions in Gaulish, dating to the later first millennium B.C.E. have been discovered in recent years in southern France, Spain, and Italy. One example is a bilingual inscription written in Gaulish and Latin found in Todi, northern Italy (Green, 1997).

One reason why written language was not common in the Celtic world is that it was believed to be inferior to storytelling from memory. Observations made by Julius Caesar in "Book VI" of his account of the Gallic Wars suggest that the Celts did not value the written word as much as they did the spoken one. The Druids prioritized learning from memory over recording facts, believing that it was easier to keep knowledge exclusive to themselves if it was memorized rather than written down (Green, 1997).

Ogham

Ogham is the earliest form of writing in Irish. The language is of linguistic rather than literary interest because it is an example of an older state of the Irish language than is found in other literary sources (MacKillop, 1998). It adapted the Latin alphabet into a series of "letters" consisting of straight lines and notches carved onto the edge of a piece of stone or wood. Calling it the Gaelic or Celtic tree alphabet is fitting because each letter is assigned a tree or plant name (Asher, 2024). Therefore, it is also indicative of how fundamental nature was in Celtic cultural discourse.

This alphabet was created in the sixth century A.D. and was used in the Gaelic kingdom of Dál Riada, located in modern-day Argyll, West

Lochaber, and the Inner Hebrides of Scotland and the northern tip of Ireland. The Celts believed that the letter system was created by Ogma, the god of rhetoric and eloquence, due to the similarity between his name and the language.

Most ogham inscriptions are very short, only consisting of a name or a patronymic intended to modify the meaning of a word. Surviving inscriptions mainly date to between the fourth and eighth centuries A.D. and are found on standing stones. There is some evidence that some may have been carved in wood, although no examples survive. Many surviving instances appear to be memorials to the dead; meanwhile, others mark a border between two lands (MacKillop, 1998).

The Romans would later introduce a more comprehensive writing system to Europe. Eventually, this led to written traditions that Christian monks brought to the former Celtic world between the fifth and seventh centuries A.D. and the High Middle Ages. In Ireland, this tradition involved recording the stories of the Druids and the mythological cycles in writing (Green, 1997). However, it was when the Celts invented and adopted ogham that they began their love affair with the written word, which would ultimately lead to their stories being recorded to be enjoyed throughout the ages.

The legacy of the Celtic tradition of the written word has long endured, as evidenced by the wealth of poets, writers, and playwrights over the centuries from Ireland. Illustrious examples include W.B. Yeats, J.M. Synge, Seamus Heaney, and John O'Donohue.

Visual Arts

Another dimension of Celtic art is the visual arts, which range from ancient cave art to the illustrations found in sacred texts made in the early medieval period after Europe had converted to Christianity. Celtic art was created across geography, time, space, and cultures. The term "Celtic art" generally refers to the cultural products of the European Iron Age, which dates from around 1000 B.C.E. until the Roman Conquest. This includes the art from the La Tène period, which was created from around the fifth to the first centuries B.C.E. onwards (Megaw & Megaw, 2001).

La Tène Art

"La Tène" is the term for the main archaeological phase of the Celtic Iron Age, and it is named after the great deposit of metalwork found with other material in the water on the margin of Lake Neuchâtel in Switzerland. This phase dates from the fifth century B.C.E. to the Roman occupation of Britain and continental Europe between the first century B.C.E. and the first century A.D. (Green, 1997).

The tradition comprises art with a unique visual composition that is also influenced by the art forms of the Mediterranean and Near Eastern worlds. The La Tène phase is known for its excellent weapons and an abundance of decorative arts. These styles were initially inspired by the Hallstatt styles and later by Illyrian/Scythian art (Mountain, 1998).

La Tène art is abstract, nonrealistic art full of energy and patterns, some of which turn into human faces and others pseudo-representational designs. It can be found all over temperate Europe, from Ireland to Romania (Green, 1997). The style is full of abstract images of plants, animals, and gods, which are often woven together and combined with scrollwork and other abstract patterning (Mountain, 1998).

Artwork in this style has been found on metalwork and pottery as well as in chariot burials (Kipfer, 2000). One example dates from the first century B.C.E. and was found in the sacred lake of Llyn Cerrig Bach in Anglesey, which may have been a Druidic holy site. The artwork is a bronze plate decorated with a bird-headed triskele, which is a three-pronged pattern radiating from a common point (Green, 1997). This example demonstrates how, in this art style, a figure (a bird) is transformed into a pattern.

Insular Art: The Book of Kells

One of the other significant artistic traditions that incorporates elements of Celtic art is the early medieval art of Britain and Ireland. From this tradition, we have *The Book of Kells* and other similar illuminated manuscripts. This is the form of art that is considered to be Celtic art by most of the English-speaking world and is known as Insular art by historians (Laing & Laing, 1992).

The Book of Kells, otherwise known as *The Book of Columba,* is an illuminated manuscript and Celtic gospel book written in Latin. It contains four gospels of the New Testament that were created in a Columban monastery in Scotland or Ireland around 800 A.D. (Claddagh Design, 2014). It is one of the best and most famous examples of a manuscript created in the Insular style, which was produced between the late sixth and early ninth centuries A.D. in monasteries in Ireland, England, and Scotland, as well as in continental monasteries with links to the Anglo-Saxon or Hiberno-Scottish worlds (Henry, 1974).

While *The Book of Kells* is mainly illustrated in a way that highlights the Biblical stories it contains, many of its design elements are reflective of early Celtic art. On each page in the manuscript, the first letter in the first word of each paragraph is much bigger than the others, and each is brightly decorated with imagery, such as people, animals, and mythical creatures. These figures can be seen performing actions, such as engaging in battle.

These designs are typical of the Celtic style. Also, the practice of illustrating the first letter of each paragraph is commonplace and unique to Irish illuminated manuscripts. Notably, *The Book of Kells* is the only example of a text produced in this way, where every opening letter has been decorated in this fashion. In similar designs, the entire pages of the manuscript are also decorated, including the headers, the margins, the spaces between paragraphs, and sometimes even the gaps between lines of text. It has been suggested that the Celtic designs found in *The Book of Kells* were inspired by a slightly older book, *The Book of Durrow*, which also contains ornamented letters that end in coiled Celtic spirals (Claddagh Designs, 2014).

Both the La Tène and the Insular styles were also influenced by non-Celtic designs. However, both are considered Celtic due to their preference for stylized geometrical decoration over figurative subjects. When narrative scenes are featured in either style, they can be attributed to an outside influence (Megaw & Megaw, 2001).

These styles are also defined by characteristics such as energetic circular forms, spirals, and triskeles. Much of the art in the La Tène style that does survive is created in precious metal, such as the four Iron Age trumpets that were discovered in a lake at Loughnashade, County Armagh, all of which were decorated in La Tène style art (Green, 1997). However, stones, high crosses, and monumental sculptures dating to the Celtic period are incredibly rare.

Modern Legacy

The Celtic emphasis on visual arts has had a continuous influence throughout European history, right up to the modern day. Some examples are the mystical paintings of Jack Butler Yeats (brother of W.B. Yeats) and the widespread popularity of Celtic motifs.

Celtic-style art was also commonplace during the Celtic Revival, which started in the 18th century and has survived into the modern era. This resurrection originated with modern Celts living mostly in the British Isles who wanted to identify with their home countries and the national traditions of Scotland, Ireland, and Wales. Due to their efforts, the Celtic style has survived into the modern era and remains popular in funerary monuments, such as Celtic crosses and interlace tattoos. Inspired by archaeological discoveries from the Celtic period, the style copies Celtic motifs, mainly from the Insular style; however, La Tène art has also influenced the Art Nouveau movement.

One example of Celtic art's modern legacy is the popularity of creating art and jewelry inspired by ancient symbols and knotwork. Celtic-style jewelry has been popular from the 1840s onward as part of the Celtic revival that has been ongoing from the late 18th century onward. This style has been inspired by archaeological finds and popularized by Scottish and Irish jewelers who excelled at creating reproductions of eighth-century A.D. Celtic body ornaments (Campbell, 2006). Today, the practice of creating Celtic jewelry is considered to be therapeutic, as it allows the individual maker to express and display their emotions through art.

Music and Song

Music

Noise, chanting, singing, dancing, and music all likely played a part in Celtic religious festivals and rituals. For example, rattles, or *sistra,* carried in processions have been discovered by archaeologists. These are bronze pole tips or wands with rings from which tiny bells are suspended. Six such "jangles" have been found at a temple in Brigstock, Northamptonshire, England. In addition, an object from a horde of sacred bronzes, found in association with a coin dated 260 A.D. in a moat at Flemington Hall in Norfolk, England, has been identified as a rattle (Green, 1997).

Music was both valued for itself and as a part of religious and spiritual activity. One example is instances where intricately designed trumpets have been discovered in Ireland. This is evidenced by one trumpet found in Ardbrinn, County Down, which was found well-preserved. The object contained over 1,000 rivets.

Another more comprehensive find was four bronze trumpets dating to the Iron Age period that were discovered in 1798 in a lake at Loughnashade, County Armagh. The trumpets were superbly crafted and beautifully decorated with La Tène designs. They were likely placed in the lake as an offering alongside human sacrifices, as human skulls were also found in the area (Green, 1997).

These instruments took time, skill, and care to create, demonstrating the value placed on music and song in Celtic culture. The existence of these rattles and trumpets is also suggestive of the role music played in ritualistic activity.

Song

The bards practiced singing while they recited poetry and told their stories. This can be determined because *bardos* means "the singer of praise to men" and also "the singer of praise to god" (Ross, 1995: 431). Significantly, one requirement of the medieval Welsh pencerdd was to sing one song to God and another to the king. This example symbolizes the ritualistic and religious dimensions of the role of storytellers in Celtic society.

Singing is alluded to by Diodorus Siculus in his *Library of History* V29 4-5 (Green, 1997: 76):

> They [the Gauls] cut off the heads of enemies slain in
> battle and attach them to the necks of their horses. The
> blood-stained spoils they hand over to their attendants and
> carry off as booty, while singing a song of victory.

Diodorus Siculus' observations suggest that singing was an important part of ritualistic activity and celebration. The bard's singing was also part of the great feasting and drinking warriors partook in. These celebrations were accompanied by songs of the glory and deeds of dead heroes and the warriors assembled (Lavin, 2011).

The dual purpose of singing for the Celts is also recorded in myth. For example, it is said that after the young warrior and musician Donn Bó was killed in battle, his head was brought to a feast where he was asked to sing. His head then proceeded to perform such a piercing melody that his music reduced everyone who heard it to tears (Monaghan, 2004). The reason for this was that Donn Bó's severed head was neither entirely of this world, nor was it part of the Otherworld, so he sang a song that belonged to a world that was not ours. This myth shows that performing songs was a way for the Celts to communicate with the departed.

The tradition of song in Celtic culture survived the end of the Celtic era and played a strong part in the Celtic Revival that began in the late 18th century. A strong interest in early Celtic literature, particularly poetry, resulted in a gathering together of verse and music by a group of Welshmen, including the harper Edward Jones, who published two important collections: *The Musical and Poetical Relics of the Welsh Bards* (1784) and *The Bardic Museum of Primitive British Literature* (1802). One of Jones' pieces, "A Druidical Song," set to harp contains the following verse (Green, 1997: 152):

The enlighten'd Crowd with grateful raptures glow,
And crown his head with Sacred Mistletoe
With Mistletoe, the leaves of Oak they bind,
And hail him Druid, friend of Human Kind,
And hail him Druid, a friend of Human Kind.

This song is demonstrative of an increased interest in Welsh history, Celtic roots, and a time when the country was independent of Britain. As such, Celtic song was a way to express national pride and nationalist sentiment.

Similar notions are expressed in modern Celtic music. This comprises a broad group of genres that have developed from the folk music traditions of the Celtic people of Northwestern Europe (Melhuish, 1998). One example is the rebel music scene, which expressed Irish nationalism in the west of Scotland in the 1990s. This is an example of how music was used to record memories of Ireland's troubled political history (Boyle, 2002). As such, this form of Celtic art demonstrates how these traditions are still used as a form of memory-making and as a means of memorializing past events today.

Music and song remain important to this day in Celtic lands, particularly Wales, with its tradition of producing opera singers and the male voice choir movement, the annual Eisteddfod music competition (claimed to be the largest cultural festival in Europe), the resurgence of interest in the Celtic harp, and the popularity of the music of the modern group, Celtic Woman.

Dance

Celtic dance forms were grounded in religious rituals. Dances were performed in an attempt to influence the supernatural and, through ritual figures and steps, gain favor and assistance from the deities (Knowles, 2002). One example of evidence that suggests that Celtic dance took place for spiritual purposes is "The Aylesford Horses," a picture of horses with human legs. Green (1997) proposes that this could be a depiction of men dressed in horse skins taking part in a ritual dance.

Dancing sometimes appears in Celtic myths and legends, and it is particularly associated with fairies. For example, fairy rings are circles in lawns or pastures thought to have been caused by the dancing of these mythical creatures (MacKillop, 1998).

Another interesting example from Irish myth is the story of Eithne (or Ethna), a young bride whose husband holds many festivals in her honor. One evening, while dancing, she falls into a swoon and visits a beautiful country to which she longs to return (MacKillop, 1998). This example suggests that the Celts believed dance was a spiritual practice that was a way of entering the Otherworld or encountering other supernatural phenomena.

Ring or circle dances were some of the earliest Celtic styles. These dances often took place around maypoles or trees because of the Celts' close affinity with nature. As sun worshippers, their dances frequently also took place around a fire. They danced clockwise in circles in celebration or counterclockwise when they were in mourning. Dance moves include stopping in one spot and repeatedly tapping the foot. Called "stepping it out," "tapping it out," or "dancing it out." These types of movements are still seen today and are precursors to solo dances that are called Irish step dances (Knowles, 2002).

Historians have suggested that there is a link between Irish dance and ancient Celtic dancing. The exact origin of Irish dancing is unknown, although some evidence does suggest that there might be a link between early forms of Celtic dance and modern Irish dance. The Celts worshipped the sun, and their pagan dances often took place within circular formations of stones that have some resemblance to the circular formation of Irish step dancing (Celtic Dance, 2024).

The first written reference to dancing in Ireland was made in 1265 A.D. during the Anglo-Norman period. It was recorded in a poem entitled "Rithmus Facture Ville de Ross" ("The Entrenchment of New Ross"):

> Then the youths advanced in turn,
> And the town they made it ring
> With their merry caroling.
> Singing loud and full of mirth.

> (Frederiksen & Li Chang, 2024: 141)

During this period, the Irish danced to carols that European invaders had brought to Ireland. However, these carols were performed in a circle, echoing beliefs about how the Celts danced either clockwise or anti-clockwise, suggesting that the formation was a reflection of ancient dancing practices.

Today, the legacy of Celtic dance survives thanks to the huge surge in popularity of modern Irish dancing, both in show spectacles such as Riverdance and on the international competition circuit. Celtic dance also manifests itself in art forms still practiced today, such as Scottish sword dancing.

Summary

This section has explored and acknowledged the importance of the arts in the Celtic world. It is apparent that the Celts valued all art forms, from music, song, and dance to storytelling and the visual arts.

This legacy survives today in the form of the active modern creative output from the populations of the Celtic lands that are becoming increasingly popular. We can take inspiration from the ancient Celts' veneration of all art forms as a way of deepening our connection to life. This is a way of challenging the elimination of the arts from school curriculums, as STEM subjects come at the expense of these creative subjects. It is imperative that we keep the arts alive from childhood onward.

What is interesting about the Celts is that they did not separate the arts from their spirituality; instead, creativity was an integral part of their spiritual life. Celtic myths and legends were remembered and transmitted from generation to generation through storytelling, poetry, and song, which were memorized by the poet class, which included bards and Druids. Music and dance formed an integral part of religious rituals, while art often decorated sacred objects or depicted spiritual themes and creatures.

This section is the last area we will be exploring in this guide to Celtic spirituality. Following on from this, the concluding section presents a summary of what this book has covered and how we can harness Celtic spirituality today to inspire our present and the future.

Chapter Six

Conclusion

On this echoing-day of your birth,
May you open the gift of solitude
In order to receive your soul;
Enter the generosity of silence
To hear your hidden heart,
Know the serenity of stillness
To be enfolded anew
By the miracle of your being.

–John O'Donohue, from *To Bless the Space Between Us: A Book of Blessings*

Our beginner's guide to Celtic spirituality is almost at an end. In the previous chapters, we have explored all the key themes that crop up in an examination of the spiritual way of life of the ancient Celtic population of Europe. More specifically, in this book, we have covered Celtic mythology and ritual, the role of nature and landscape, the role of animals in the Celtic belief system, the role of the Divine Feminine in the Celtic tradition, and the sacred nature of art and its role in Celtic religious practice.

The fascinating thing about Celtic spirituality is that it is a realm not entirely separate from the secular world. While we have created divisions between nature and urban living and the secular and the sacred in the modern world, to the Celts they were all one.

One notable example is the form of the Celtic gods. Historians have speculated that the Celtic gods were not human in form; instead, they were sometimes forces of nature, such as lakes or trees. In Celtic myth, we also see that some of the gods, such as the Morrígan, have the power to transform themselves into birds or animals, also demonstrating how different beings were closely linked to one another.

Furthermore, even the Celts' afterlife was not entirely separate from the physical realm, as their myths and legends tell us of how spirits visited Earth and how living humans visited the Otherworld and returned from it.

This theme of the spiritual world being linked to the physical one is something that we can incorporate into our lives today. Celtic spirituality reminds us of how we have lost our fundamental link to nature and the living world around us, so by understanding and appreciating it once more, we can get that back.

One method for how you can do this might be through singing. The next time you sing, whether it be at a karaoke night or just in the shower, think of how the Celts saw song as a link between this realm and the next, how in myth they talked of the song of the Otherworld sounding more beautiful and moving than anything else we have ever heard. So, when you sing, you are communicating with the spiritual realm.

Other ways of keeping Celtic traditions alive include observing the Celtic festivals of the year, undertaking creative arts pursuits, going on pilgrimages to sacred sites, or paying closer and more mindful attention on walks in local beauty spots. More fundamentally, consider taking the lessons of the ancient Celts and their deep respect for the surrounding world to aid a more profound understanding of our stewardship of the land and our responsibility toward keeping it alive at this critical point in time.

Key Takeaways

Each chapter has had a key takeaway that reflects the overarching theme of the book.

Chapter 1: Celtic Mythology and Ritual

Chapter 1 looked into the Celtic religion, its gods, and its belief systems. Of particular interest were the spiritual rituals the Celts practiced to mark the passing of one season of the year to the next. Because a good season and a strong harvest were key to their survival, these celebrations demonstrate how the Celts were profoundly invested in the natural phases of the calendar.

In the first chapter, we also explored how we can include Celtic religious rituals into our everyday lives in a way that allows us to appreciate the spiritual dimension of our existence. One example is the Celtic practice of greeting the sun and the sunrise each morning, which encourages us to be grateful for the beginning of each day.

Chapter 2: Nature and Landscape

Chapter 2 explored the strong connection the Celts enjoyed with nature. It also looked at the significance of particular natural elements in the Celtic worldview, such as trees and water. It also delved into how nature inspired mythic figures such as the fairies, giants, and kelpies that appear in Celtic folklore. The Celts also saw nature as a healing force, and it had a key influence on their religious calendar, as we discovered.

In this chapter, we also considered the origin of the Celtic sacred sites such as Stonehenge. We learned of the many fairy circles found in Ireland that survive into the present day and that we can make journeys to visit to honor the Celtic past.

Chapter 3: The Animal Kingdom

Chapter 3 considered the significance of the animal kingdom to the Celts. Animals were valuable to these ancient societies, as they sustained and assisted humans. The value animals had is demonstrated by the role that they played in Celtic religious traditions, such as the practice of animal sacrifice as a way of honoring the gods in the hope of them bestowing good fortune on worshippers.

Animals also appeared in Celtic mythology and folklore, symbolizing different themes and characteristics. For example, a warrior going into battle might wear a motif of an animal with fearsome qualities on their armor. In doing so, they expressed their hope that they might also demonstrate some of the same qualities as that creature on the battlefield.

The strong bond the Celts developed with animals survives into the present day through the ways we love and cherish our pets. Like the Celts, we can also learn from our nonhuman companions and be inspired by their better qualities.

Chapter 4: The Divine Feminine in Celtic Tradition

Chapter 4 looked at the power and influence Celtic women enjoyed and how they had a far more influential and prominent position in society than their contemporaries in ancient Greece and Rome. Women were also closely associated with spiritual power in Celtic culture. This is where the Divine Feminine comes in, which is a soft, nurturing, empowering energy typically associated with women. Its opposite is the Divine Masculine. Both forms of energy are needed by us all to achieve inner balance.

This chapter further considered ways in which the Celts valued the Divine Feminine through an exploration of examples found in history and legend. It also looked at the kinds of divine powers historically attributed to Celtic women and the concept of spiritual warriorship. We further noted that these divinely feminine qualities can be nurtured and developed by us all today.

Chapter 5: The Arts as Sacred

Chapter 5 explored the link between the arts and spirituality in the Celtic world. In this chapter, we learned that activities such as music, song, and dance brought the Celts closer to the spirit world and that their religious belief, histories, myths, and legends were preserved through the practice of storytelling. This was often expressed in the form of poetry or song. The visual arts also served to vividly illustrate the Celtic world and their beliefs. From these findings, it is possible to consider how, today, Celtic storytelling survives in the form of the practice of spoken-word storytelling and how the arts form a link between the physical and spiritual worlds.

What This Means for the Present and the Future

"All things are inconstant except the faith in the soul, which changes all things and fills their inconstancy with light" (James Joyce, writing to Lady Gregory, November 1902).

From what we have learned about Celtic spirituality, the overarching point is to be inspired to value the natural world and the spiritual connections that exist between humanity and all living beings and things in the present and the future. This is particularly important given the current state of the environmental crisis. We can use the Celts' ancient wisdom to value and cherish the world we live in, attempting to live in a way that honors nature rather than destroys it.

The way in which Celtic rituals honor nature, placing emphasis and value on the passing of time, is a wonderful starting point for learning to cherish the world around us. By drawing connections between the past and the present, we can utilize the best of ancient Celtic spiritual wisdom to greatly enrich the way we live our lives today.

If you have enjoyed reading this book, it would be greatly appreciated if you would take a moment to give it a quick review and rating on Amazon. This is so helpful in boosting its visibility.

To make this quick and easy for you, just scan the QR code of your country's Amazon marketplace.

Many thanks again for choosing to read this book, and please keep your eye out for upcoming books in this series.

Neve Sullivan
www.nevesullivan.com

US: Leave a review on amazon.com:

UK: Leave a review on amazon.co.uk:

AUSTRALIA: Leave a review on amazon.com.au:

CANADA: Leave a review on amazon.ca:

About the Author

Neve Sullivan's interest in ancient history and mythology is deeply rooted in her academic background and extensive travels around the world. She holds a BA Honors degree and a postgraduate diploma. Neve's dissertation focused on the cultural identity of Celtic lands, and in it, she examined the Celts' unique expression through their literature, storytelling, poetry, song, and painting.

Neve's professional career in archives has led to a deep appreciation for historical texts and artifacts. She believes that understanding our historical roots enhances our appreciation for nature, brings magic into everyday life, and helps us value the arts as an integral part of our cultural identity.

Her books aim to help modern readers reconnect with ancient wisdom in a context that resonates with them, bridge gaps between past traditions and present realities, and remind us that there are timeless truths rooted in our history that still hold relevance today. Discover a new perspective on life and history with Neve Sullivan's series *Celtic Wisdom for Modern Life*.

COMING SOON by Neve Sullivan:
A Beginner's Guide to Celtic Mythology: *An introduction to the mysteries and magic of Celtic legend and lore.*

www.nevesullivan.com

References and Bibliography

Alberro, M. (2005). Celtic legacy in Galicia. *E-Keltoi: Journal of Interdisciplinary Celtic Studies, 6*: 1005-1035.

Armitage, J. (2020). *Celtic queen: The world of Cartimandua*. Amberley.

Asher, H. (2023). *The importance of nature connection in Celtic culture: Exploring animism and Celtic beliefs*.
An Darach.
https://silvotherapy.co.uk/articles/nature-connection-celts

Asher, H. (2024). *The ogham alphabet*. An Darach. https://silvotherapy.co.uk/gaelic-tree-alphabet

AVMA. (2024). *Human-animal bond*. American Veterinary Medical Association. https://www.avma.org/one-health/human-animal-bond

Barber, N. (2014). The way they never were: Nationalism, landscape, and the myth in Irish identity construction
[Master of Arts Thesis, Georgia State University].
ScholarWorks @ Georgia State University. https://scholarworks.gsu.edu/rs_theses/47/

Beda, V. (1999). *Bede, the reckoning of time*. Liverpool University Press.

Berg, S. (2022). *Brigid: The Celtic goddess who became a saint*. Creek Ridge Publishing.

Bittarello, M. B. (2008). Reading texts, watching texts: Mythopoesis on neopagan websites. D. Llewellyn & D. F. Sawyer (Eds.). *Reading spiritualities: Constructing and representing the sacred*. Ashgate.

Bonewits, I. (2006). *Bonewits's essential guide to Druidism*. Kensington.

Boyle, M. (2002). Edifying the rebellious Gael: Uses of memories of Ireland's troubled past among the West of Scotland's Irish Catholic diaspora. In D. C. Harvey, R. Jones, & N. McInroy (Eds.). *Celtic geographies: Old culture, new times*. Routledge.

Brunner, C. F. (2015). *Mountain magic: Celtic shamanism in the Austrian Alps*. Lulu.com

Burkeman, O. (2014). *This column will change your life: Where Heaven and Earth collide*. The Guardian. https://www.theguardian.com/life-andstyle/2014/mar/22/this-column-change-your-life-heaven-earth

Burl, A., (2000). *The stone circles of Britain, Ireland, and Brittany*. Yale University Press.

Butser Ancient Farm. (2024). *Celtic fire festival: Burning the Wickerman*. https://www.butserancientfarm.co.uk/beltain-celtic-fire-festival

Byghan, Y. (2020). *Sacred and mythological animals: A worldwide taxonomy*. McFarland & Company.

Byrnes, M. (2005). Feis. In S. Duffy (Ed.). *Medieval Ireland: An encyclopedia*. Routledge.

Caesar, C. J. (2022). *De Bello Gallico and other commentaries*. Aegitas.

Califia, T. (2012). *Initiate: A witch's circle of water*. Llewellyn Publications.

Campbell, G. (Ed.). (2006). *The Grove encyclopedia of decorative arts*. Oxford University Press.

Carr-Gomm, P., & Carr-Gomm, S. (1994). *The Druid animal oracle: Working with the sacred animals of the Druid tradition*. Connections.

Carroll, R. (2018). *Spoken word poets and rappers inject new energy into an Irish tradition*. The Guardian. https://www.theguardian.com/world/2018/dec/24/spoken-word-poets-inject-energy-irish-tradition-storytelling

Cartwright, M. (2021a). *Sacred sites & rituals in the ancient Celtic religion*. World History Encyclopedia. https://www.worldhistory.org/article/1710/sacred-sites--rituals-in-the-ancient-celtic-religi/

Cartwright, M. (2021b). *Death, burial, & the afterlife in the ancient Celtic religion*. World History Encyclopedia. https://www.worldhistory.org/article/1707/death-burial--the-afterlife-in-the-ancient-celtic/

Celtic Steps. (2024). *The history of Irish dance*. https://celtic-steps.ie/our-story/the-history-of-irish-song-music-dance/

Chadwick, N. K. (1970). *The Celts.* Penguin.

Circle Sanctuary. (2023). *Beltane.* https://www.circlesanctuary.org/beltane

Citizen Ticket. (2024). *Beltane fire festival 2024.* Beltane Fire Society. https://www.citizenticket.com/events/beltane-fire-society/beltane-fire-festival-2024-1/

Claddagh Design. (2014). *Irish treasures: The Book of Kells.* https://www.claddaghdesign.com/en-gb/blogs/irish-interest/irish-treasures-the-book-of-kells

Condren, M. (1989). *The serpent and the goddess: Women, religion, and power in Celtic Ireland.* Harper & Row.

Cunliffe B. (1997). *The ancient Celts.* Oxford University Press.

Davidson, H. E. (1988). *Myths and symbols in Pagan Europe: Early Scandinavian and Celtic Religions.* Syracuse University Press.

Davies, J. A. (2008). *The land of Boudica: Prehistoric and Roman Norfolk.* Oxford Books.

Davies, O. (1999). *Celtic spirituality.* Paulist Press.

Duncan, G. (2015). Celtic spirituality and the environment. *HTS Theological Studies, 71*(1) https://www.scielo.org.za/scielo.php?script=sci_arttext&pid=S0259-94222015000200069

The Editors of Encyclopaedia Britannica, (2023). *Cernunnos.* Britannica. https://www.britannica.com/topic/Cernunnos

The Editors of Encylopaedia Britannica. (2024a). *Esus.* Britannica. https://www.britannica.com/topic/Esus

The Editors of Encyclopedia Britannica. (2024b). *Bran.* Britannica. https://www.britannica.com/topic/Bran-Celtic-god

Ellis, P.B. (1999). *The chronicles of the Celts: New tellings of their myths & legends.* Carroll & Graf Publishers, Inc.

Frederiksen, L. E., & Li Chang, S. M. (Eds.). (2024). *Dance cultures around the world.* Human Kinetics.

Gamkrelidze, T. V., & Ivanov, V. V. (1995). *Indo-European and the Indo-Europeans: A reconstruction and historical analysis of a proto-language and proto-culture.* Walter de Gruyter.

Gargarin, M. (2010). *The Oxford encyclopedia of ancient Greece and Rome: Vol. 1.* Oxford University Press.

Good, K. (2021). *10 important life lessons we can learn from animals.* Our Green Planet. https://www.onegreenplanet.org/animalsandnature/important-life-lessons-we-can-learn-from-animals/

The Goodness Project. (2024). *These vegan statistics prove veganism is only getting started.* https://thegoodnessproject.co.uk/blog/vegan-statistics

Grace, L. (2022). *Pagan Britain: The UK's ancient sacred sites.* Horizon Guides.
https://horizonguides.com/journal/pagan-uk

Green, M. (1989). *Symbol & image in Celtic religious art.* Routledge.

Green, M. (1998). *Animals in Celtic life and myth.* Routledge.

Green, M. A. (2011). *The gods of the Celts.* The History Press.

Green, M. J. (1992). The early Celts. In G. Price (Ed.). *The Celtic connection.* Colin Smythe.

Green, M. J. (1997). *Exploring the world of the Druids.* Thames & Hudson.

Greene, D., Thomson, D. S., & Jones, T. (2024). *Celtic literature.* Britannica. https://www.britannica.com/art/Celtic-literature

Harris, K. A., Panzica, K. M., & Crocker, R. A. (2016). Paganism and counseling: The development of a clinical resource. Open Theology. 859. 10.1515/opth-2016-0065

Henry, F. (1974). *The Book of Kells: Reproductions from the manuscript in Trinity College, Dublin.* Alfred A. Knopf.

Heinz, S. (2010). Afterlife and Celtic concepts of the otherworld. In L. Sikorska (Ed.). *Thise stories beren witnesse: The landscape of the afterlife in medieval and post-medieval imagination.* Peter Lang.

Hutton, R. (1993). *The pagan religions of the ancient British Isles.* Blackwell.

Hutton, R. (1996). *The stations of the sun: A history of ritual year in Britain.* Blackwell.

Irby-Massie, G. L. (1999). *Military religion in Roman Britain.* Brill.

Johnson, A. (2008). *Solving Stonehenge: The new key to an ancient enigma.* Thames & Hudson.

Johnson, B. (2024). *Glastonbury, Somerset.* Historic

UK. https://www.historic-uk.com/HistoryMagazine/Destinations UK/Glastonbury/

Jufer, N., & Luginbuhl, T. (2001). *Les dieux gaulois: Repertoire des noms de divinites celtiques connus par l'epigraphie, les textes antiques et la toponymie*. Editions Errance.

King, A. (1990). *Roman Gaul and Germany*. The University of California Press.

Kipfer, B. A. (2000). *Encyclopedic dictionary of archaeology*. Kluwer Academic.

Knowles, M. (2002). *Tap roots: The early history of tap dancing*. McFarland & Company.

Koch, J. (2006). *Celtic culture: A historical encyclopedia*. ABC-CLIO.

Laing, L., & Laing, J. (1992). *Art of the Celts*. Thames & Hudson.

Laurie, E. R., O'Morrighu, A. R., Machate, J., Price, K. T., & Lambert ni Dhoireann, K. (2005). Celtic reconstructionist paganism. In P. Telesco. (Ed.). *Which witch is which?* New Page Books/The Career Press.

Lavin, P. (2011). *The shaping of the Celtic world: And the resurgence of the Celtic consciousness in the 19th and 20th centurie*s. iUniverse.

Leslie, C. W., & Gerace, F. E. (2000). *The ancient Celtic festivals and how we celebrate them today*. Simon & Schuster.

Littlefield, C. (2005). *Rekindling an ancient faith*. Las Vegas Sun. https://lasvegassun.com/news/2005/nov/08/rekindling-an-ancient-faith/

Lynch, F. (1970). *Prehistoric Anglesey*. Anglesey Antiquarian Society.

Lynch, D. (2023). *Have we reached the end of nature? Our relationship with the environment is in crisis*. The Conversation. https://theconversation.com/have-we-reached-the-end-of-nature-our-relationship-with-the-environment-is-in-crisis-206278

Lysaght, P. (1999). Traditional storytelling in Ireland in the twentieth century. In M. R. MacDonald (Ed.). *Traditional storytelling today: An international sourcebook*. Routledge.

MacBain, A. (1976). *Celtic mythology and religion*. Folcroft Library Editions.

MacCulloch, J. A. (1911). *The religion of the ancient Celts*. T&T Clark.

MacCulloch, J. A. Rolleston, T. W., and Evans-Wentz, W. Y. (2023). *Celtic mythology*. DigiCat.

MacEowen, F. (2007). *The Celtic way of seeing: Meditations on the Irish spirit wheel*. New World Library.

MacKillop, J. (1998). *Dictionary of Celtic mythology*. Oxford University Press.

MacNeill, M., (1962). *The festival of Lughnasa: A study of the survival of the Celtic festival of the beginning of harvest*. Oxford University Press.

Magan, M. (2017). Fairy forts: Why these "sacred places" deserve our respect. *The Irish Times*. https://www.irishtimes.com/culture/heritage/fairy-forts-why-these-sacred-places-deserve-our-respect-1.3181259

Mallory, J. P., & Adams, D. Q. (2006). *The Oxford introduction to Proto-Indo-European and the Proto-Indo-European world*. Oxford University Press.

Marzluff, J. M., & Angell, T. (2007). *In the company of crows and ravens*. Yale University Press.

McColman, C. (2003). *The complete idiot's guide to Celtic wisdom*. Alpha Press.

McColman, C. (2024). *Contemplation and Celtic spirituality*. Anamchara. https://anamchara.com/unknowing/celtic-contemplation/

McCoppin, R. S. (2023). *Goddess lost: How the downfall of female deities degraded women's status in world cultures*. McFarland & Company.

McCoy, E. (1995). *Celtic myth & magick: Harness the power of the gods and goddesses*. Llewellyn Publications.

McQuillan, S. (2024). Celtic ritual & May dew. *Linked Magazine*. https://linkedmagazine.co.uk/celtic-ritual-may-dew/

Megaw, R., & Megaw, V. (2001). *Celtic art: From its beginnings to the Book of Kells*. Thames & Hudson.

Melhuish, M. (1998). *Celtic tides: Traditional music in a new age*. Quarry Press, Inc.

Michigan State University. (2018). The human-animal bond throughout time. https://cvm.msu.edu/news/perspectives-magazine/perspectives-fall-2018/the-human-animal-bond-throughout-time

Miller, D.A. (1998). On the mythology of Indo-European heroic hair. *Journal of Indo-European Studies, 26*(1-2): 41-60.

Milligan, M. (2021). *10 British Iron Age hill forts*. Heritage Daily. https://www.heritagedaily.com/2021/03/10-british-iron-age-hill-forts/118900

Monaghan, P. (2004). *The encyclopedia of Celtic mythology and folklore*. Facts on File.

Morris, M. (2008). *A great and terrible king: Edward I and the forging of Britain*. Hutchinson.

Mountain, H. (1998). *The Celtic encyclopedia*. Universal Publishers.

National Trust. (2024). *History of giant's causeway*. https://www.nationaltrust.org.uk/visit/northern-ireland/giants-causeway/history-of-giants-causeway

NicMhacha, S. M. (2005). *Queen of the night: Rediscovering the Celtic moon goddess*. Weiser Books.

Niemchick, A., & Rogers, K. (2023). *Celtic region: Beliefs, practices, and institutions*. Britannica. https://www.britannica.com/topic/human-body-systems-2237111

O'Donohue, J. (1999). Anam Cara: Spiritual wisdom from the Celtic world. Bantam.

O'Donohue, J. (2000). Eternal Echoes: Exploring Our Hunger To Belong. Bantam.

O'Giollain, D. (1991). *The good people: New Fairylore essays*. Garland.

O'Hara, K. (2023). *11 major Celtic gods and goddesses (2024)*. The Irish Road Trip. https://www.theirishroadtrip.com/celtic-gods-and-goddesses/

O'Sullivan, B. (2024). *The surprising truth about Irish women warriors*. Irish Imbas. https://irishimbasbooks.com/the-surprising-truth-about-irish-women-warriors/

Oleszkiewicz-Peralba, M. (2009). *The black madonna in Latin America and Europe*. University of New Mexico Press.

Olmsted, G. S. (1976). The Gundestrup version of *Tain Bo Cuailnge*. *Antiquity, 50*(198): 95-103.

Oxford Reference. (2024). *Ogmios*. A Dictionary of Celtic Mythology. https://www.oxfordreference.com/display/10.1093/oi/authority.20110803100247137

Paterson, H. (1997). *The handbook of Celtic astrology: The 13-sign lunar zodiac of the ancient Druids*. Llewellyn Publications.

Pennington, R. (2003). *Amazons and fighter pilots: A biographical dictionary of military women*. Greenwood Press.

Powell, T. G. E. (1958). *The Celts*. Thames & Hudson.

Prabhat, S. (2011). *Difference between fairy and faerie. DifferenceBetween .net*. http://www.differencebetween.net/language/words-language/difference-between-fairy-and-faerie/

Puhvel, J. (1981). Aspects of equine functionality. *Analecta Indoeuropaea*. 159–172.

Roman Britain. (2024). *Animals in Celtic mythology*. https://www.roman-britain.co.uk/the-celts-and-celtic-life/animals-in-celtic-mythology/

Ross, A. (1967). *Pagan Celtic Britain: Studies in iconography and tradition*. Sphere Books Ltd.

Ross, A. (1972). *Everyday life of the pagan Celts*. Carousel Books.

Ross, A. (1995). Ritual and the Druids. In M.J. Green, (Ed.). *The Celtic world*. Routledge.

Sermon, R. (2022). Eostre and the Matronae Austriahenae. *Folklore*, *133*(2): 139–157.

Starza, L. (2023). *Pagan portals—rounding the wheel of the year: Celebrating the seasons in ritual, magic, folklore, and nature*. John Hunt Publishing.

Stead, I.M., Bourke, J.B., & Brothwell, D.R. (1986). *Lindow man: The body in the bog*. Trustees of the British Museum.

Strabone, J. (2018). *Poetry and British nationalisms in the bardic eighteenth century: Imagined antiquities*. Palgrave Macmillan.

Trees for Life. (2023). Salmon mythology and folklore. https://treesforlife.org.uk/into-the-forest/trees-plants-animals/others/salmon/salmon-mythology-and-folklore/

Vandrei, M. (2018). *Queen Boudica and historical culture in Britain: An image of truth.* Oxford University Press.

Waldman, C., & Mason, C. (2006). *Encyclopedia of European peoples.* Facts On File.

Watts, D. (2005). *Boudicca's heirs: Women in early Britain.* Routledge.

West, M. L. (2007). *Indo-European poetry and myth.* Oxford University Press.

Whitaker, M. (2023). *Imagine living well with perspective and perseverance: Book 3, Vol. v.* Fulton Books.

Williams, L. (2013). *Paganism, part 3: The Wheel of the Year.* The Guardian. https://www.theguardian.com/commentis-free/2013/jul/29/paganism-part-3-wheel-year-dates

Williams ab Ithel, J. (1874), *The Bardo-Druidic system of the Isle of Britain with translations and notes.* Bernard Quaritch.

Wilson, E. O. (2017). *Half-earth: Our planet's fight for life.* Liveright Publishing Corporation.

Wood, J. (2000). Introduction. In C. Squire (Ed.). *The mythology of the British Isles: An introduction to Celtic myth, legend, poetry, and romance.* UCL & Wordsworth.

The World Bank. (2023). *Urban development.* https://www.worldbank.org/en/topic/urbandevelopment/overview

Zell-Ravenheart, O., & Zell-Ravenheart, M. G. (2006). *Creating circles & ceremonies: Rituals for all seasons and reasons.* Career Press.

Made in the USA
Las Vegas, NV
30 May 2025

22915227R00080